The Early Etruscans

Endpapers Wall painting from the Tomb of
Hunting and Fishing, Tarquinia

LIFE IN ANCIENT LANDS
Edited by Edward Bacon

The
Early Etruscans

Donald Strong

G. P. Putnam's Sons New York

This book was designed and produced by George Rainbird Ltd,
Marble Arch House, 44 Edgware Road, London w2,
for G. P. Putnam's Sons,
200 Madison Avenue,
New York, N.Y. 10016.

The text was filmset in Great Britain by
Oliver Burridge Filmsetting Ltd, Crawley.
The book was printed and bound in Yugoslavia.

Library of Congress Catalog Card Number: 68-25457

CONTENTS

COLOR PLATES

FOREWORD

The world as we know it is a man-made world. Hardly any part of the habitable globe is unaffected by man's activity; even some of the parts which are uninhabitable were made so by man. And man himself is very largely a man-made creature; his habits, his thoughts, his memory, his aspirations are the modified sum of his ancestors' experiences.

All men are brothers, say the missionary and the idealist. True, but there is more to it than that: all men, living and dead, since the beginning of time, are our brothers; and all history is family history. The Magdalenian artist of 17,000 years ago who decorated the caves of Lascaux with bulls and horses, the Cretan who applauded the bull-leapers, the Egyptian who drew funny hippopotamuses on pieces of stone, the boy Inca who triumphed in the initiation tests, the Etruscans who delighted so frankly in wine, women and song – these are as real to us, as near to us and as sustaining to us as, at any rate, some of those who live in our own street, village, town. Or they can be.

Aristotle said that the object of poetry was pleasure. And when he used these words, he doubtless used them in the widest possible sense: poetry, to include the full range of man's creative imagination; pleasure, to encompass everything from the baby's first chuckle to the philosopher's cry of delight at apprehending a new facet of truth. Education and the pursuit of knowledge have two objectives: pleasure and power. And of these the greater is pleasure: power is transitory, pleasure is permanent.

If these books enable anyone to pass an examination, to secure a job or to dominate a competitor or friend, they will have served a purpose of a sort. Their main objective, however, is to increase the sum of human pleasure, to enlarge the circle of friendship, love and knowledge, and to present a picture of life.

Like the Philistines, the Etruscans live principally in the annals of their enemies, Etruscan history being mainly the partial records of the Romans, who saw as little reason as the Israelites for admiring their enemies. It is, then, thanks to the Romans (and also to the fatal forcefulness of Lord Macaulay), that Lars Porsena and "false Tarquin" are the classic type of Etruscan. And yet the learned Emperor Claudius (the James I of his time) wrote a history of the Etruscans – which, alas, has not survived; and the great Maecenas, the archetypal patron of the arts, friend of Virgil and Horace and Augustus, was himself an Etruscan. But their own literature, which surely must have existed in a race so cultured and so closely in touch with classical Greece, has not survived. Their brief inscriptions can, after a fashion, be read; the letters, the words, and often the meaning are intelligible, but little grammar and less syntax can be synthesised; and such Etruscan voices as come through are faint and illusory.

However, mystery is the chief spur to detection; and the great detectives of our time, the archaeologists, daily uncover more and more of the heritage of the Etruscans – their painted tombs, their terracotta sarcophagi, their strange and splendid bronzes, their painted pottery which they both made and imported from Greece – such things and many like them combine, and the shadowy features of the Etruscans emerge into the light – merchants, metal-workers, art-lovers, town-planners, mystical prognosticators, and cheerful and convivial *hommes moyen sensuels* – if we are to believe D. H. Lawrence's brilliant evocation: the best-integrated of the ancients.

EDWARD BACON

INTRODUCTION

Anyone who sets out to write a book in English about the Etruscans is conscious that he cannot match the wonderful introduction which George Dennis wrote to the second edition of *Cities and Cemeteries of Etruria* in 1878. He cannot hope to write so well, nor can he write with the confidence of what Dennis calls "the quickened energy of the nineteenth century". There is scarcely any aspect of Etruscan history and life on which a modern writer would be prepared to speak with Dennis's conviction, for he is more than conscious of the inadequacy of those "purer founts of historical truth" on which Dennis relied. The twentieth century has, it is true, made solid advances in all branches of Etruscan studies, but the chief advance has been a highly critical reassessment of the foundations of our knowledge. The modern student may be said to have replaced Dennis's confidence in the present with a confidence in the future; he feels that he has stripped the Etruscans of the prejudices of ancient and modern criticism and that future research, aided by modern scientific techniques, will answer questions which have long remained unanswered or have never before been clearly formulated.

In the next few years we can expect rapid advances in every branch of Etruscan studies. There is now, for the first time, a planned programme of research and excavation on at least some of the chief cities of Etruria, and the territories of the city-states are being surveyed by air photography and archaeological field-work, making use of modern geophysical techniques. From the excavation of the cities we may hope for, at least, a few historical documents of importance; the recent excavation in the sanctuary of Pyrgi yielded the now famous gold plaques which introduced a new historical personality, one of the rulers of Caere in the fifth century B.C. We can expect as much if not more from the excavations of Rusellae, Vulci or Vetulonia, and as more and more existing inscriptions are read, new historical facts will surely emerge. The Etruscans may never enter into the full light of history, but the progress of archaeology will enable us to test more thoroughly the validity of our present historical tradition, derived as it is from Greek and Roman sources which are fundamentally alien, if not always unfavourable.

The time has not yet come, therefore, when we can give a thoroughly convincing account of the life and times of the ancient Etruscans. This book has no claims to do so; it merely attempts to state something of what is known or can reasonably be conjectured about the structure of their society and their way of life. It differs from most modern books in being concerned only with a limited period of Etruscan history. The Etruscans apparently believed that different peoples were allotted an existence of pre-determined duration and they allowed themselves eight or ten *saecula* (a length of time variously calculated at 100 or 110 years). An ancient commentator on Virgil, known as Daniel's Servius, tells us that the comet which appeared at the time of Julius Caesar's death in 44 B.C. marked the end of their ninth *saeculum*. By that time Etruria had ceased to exist as an historical entity and the great Etruscan cities had long since fallen to Rome. Their period of splendour had been confined to not much more than three *saecula*. If we are to illustrate the life of an ancient people we must try to see them at the height of their achievement, as we might choose the days of Pericles to illustrate the life of the Athenians. This book, therefore, will be concerned only with the period which saw the rise of Etruscan civilization, the maximum extension of its power and influence, and the beginning of its decline; the years from about 750 B.C. to about 400 B.C.

B.C.	ETRURIA & ETRUSCAN COLONIES	SOUTH ITALY, SICILY AND CARTHAGE	GREECE AND IONIA
900	Archaic (Villanovan) I Iron Age occupation of Etruscan sites		
800		Founding of Carthage	
	Archaic (Villanovan) II (c.750) Beginning of foreign contacts; importation of Greek pottery	Colonization of Cumae (c.750) Colonization of Syracuse (734) Colonization of Sybaris (721)	Aristocratic government in Greek city-states
700		Colonization of Zancle (690)	
	Archaic (Villanovan) III (c.675) Rise of the Etruscan city-states Regolini-Galassi Tomb (c.650)		Tyranny of Cypselids at Corinth (c.650)
600	Tarquin dynasty in Rome Etruscan colonization of Campania	Colonization of Massalia by Phocaeans (c.600) Rise to power of Carthage Conflict between Greeks and Carthaginians in Sicily	Solon's reforms at Athens (594) Tyranny of Pisistratids at Athens (561)
	Phocaean settlement at Alalia (c.560)		
	Battle of Alalia (535) Defeat of Etruscans by Aristodemus of Cumae (524) Etruscan colonization of Po valley	Carthage completes conquest of Sardinia (c.520) Destruction of Sybaris (510)	Persian domination of Ionia (546)
500	Expulsion of Tarquins from Rome	Defeat of Carthaginians at Himera (480)	Democracy at Athens (508) Ionian Revolt (499) Battle of Marathon (490) Battle of Salamis (480) Founding of the Delian League (477)
	Defeat of Etruscans at Cumae (474) Syracusan expeditions against Etruria (453)		
	Fall of Capua (432)	Colonization of Thurii (443)	Thirty Years' Peace (443) Peloponnesian War (431–404)
		Athenian expedition to Syracuse (415) Carthaginian expedition to Sicily (409) Peace between Syracuse and Carthage (405)	
	Gauls invade N. Italy Siege of Veii (405)		
400			
	Veii falls to Romans (396)		

Chapter One

LAND

The homeland of the Etruscans is defined by clear-cut natural boundaries. The frontier on the east and south is the river Tiber with the Apennine mountains, the backbone of Italy, beyond it on the east. To the north, the natural boundary is the north-west extension of the Apennines, the so-called Apuan Alps, which run parallel to the Arno, enclosing the valley of the river and its tributaries, but the extent of early Etruscan settlement north of the river is not clearly known. Under the Roman Republic, the frontier of the region called Etruria was established with Pisa on the Arno as the northernmost town; later it was extended up to the river Magra on which the fine harbour of Luna stands. Luna may well have been used as a harbour by the Etruscans in the great days of their maritime trade, and they probably exploited the rich plains on the north side of the Arno as far as the mountain zone, though they may never have held them easily against the rugged, warlike Ligurians. The Tyrrhenian Sea, with a coastline extending some 250 miles from the Magra to the Tiber, is the western limit of Etruria.

Within its frontiers, which include all modern Tuscany and parts of Umbria and Latium, Etruria is segmental in shape, its maximum width approximately half the length of its coastline. In general character the whole region is mountainous or hilly; but with strikingly different landscapes in the south and the north. In the north-east the tracts of country immediately below the High Apennines are very mountainous; westwards, south of the Arno, runs a broad belt of hilly country known as the Sub-Apennine, enclosing fertile valleys and reaching out to include the massive volcanic cone of Monte Amiata which rises nearly 6,000 feet, just south of Siena. Below a line joining Chiusi and the promontory of Piombino is the volcanic zone of southern Etruria, a striking contrast with the valleys and mountains of the north. On its northern edge are the cones of Monte Cetona and Monte Amiata, extinct since historical times like all the volcanoes of the area. Farther south, from the Fiora to the Tiber, is the volcanic zone of modern Lazio with its picturesque tufa rocks, its deep-cut gorges and thick undergrowth. The wooded Ciminian heights bound its northern view and in its heart is the great crater of Lake Bolsena.

The flat coastal tracts of Etruria known as the Maremma begin a little to the north of Volterra and extend south to the Tiber: a succession of low-lying river basins between ranges of hills running towards the sea. This coastal region is the only part of ancient Etruria that has changed greatly since the great days of the Etruscans. The typical alternation of high coastline and low coastal plain combined with strong northward coastal currents has resulted in a steady build-up of soil in the low-lying lands. The process has been accentuated by the large-scale deforestation, an historical phenomenon which has contributed to the formation of the deltas of the Arno, the Cecina, the

Ombrone and the Tiber rivers. With the deltas came lagoons, stagnant pools and eventually malarial swamps which gave the whole coastline an unhealthy reputation since Roman times; it has only recently been reclaimed. But in Etruscan days the processes were in their early stages; the coastline was certainly more deeply indented and, though there were few good natural harbours, there were plenty of deep gulfs with respectable moorings for ships.

The great valleys of the Arno and the Tiber are the keys to the geography of Etruria. Both rivers rise in the central ridge of the Apennines and run parallel as far as Arezzo where the Arno branches westwards and the Tiber pursues its way to the south. The smaller rivers flow into the Arno or the Tiber or run west to the Tyrrhenian Sea. From the point where the Arno diverges from the Tiber the remarkable plain of the Val di Chiana, rather like a wide alluvial plain, extends south to Chiusi with only the slightest fall. Most of the rivers running down from the hills, like the Ombrone and the Albegna in the west, are rushing torrents in winter and dry, or almost dry, in summer; the tufa country of the extreme south is cut by numerous deep gorges carved out by these winter streams. The rivers and streams are the basis of the system of communications in country where, before the Romans drove through their military roads, travel was always difficult. The Tiber valley provided the main route from north to south and the river would take boats of shallow draught as far up as Orte; the valley of the Arno with its tributaries formed the chief communication system for the northern states. Near the coast the narrow plains afforded easy access between several of the chief city-states and the valleys of the little rivers penetrated inland, like the Marta which takes the surplus water of Bolsena and flows past Tarquinia. External communications were dominated by the Tiber crossings on the south and east and by the passes over the Apennines to the north; control of these external communications was always a factor of great importance in the history of Etruria.

The patterns of settlement, to a large extent dictated by nature, differed considerably in north and south. North of Bolsena, in the hills and broad valleys of modern Tuscany, the communities were more widely spread, and when towns developed they occupied the high ground on the edge of the valleys by the old ridgeway tracks that communicated between them. The south is adapted to small settlements closer to one another and usually on elevated sites chosen for defence and to avoid the winter inundations; later, several villages might be joined in a communal centre but the village community remained the basis of the political and social organization. The difficulties of inland communication, as in Greece, encouraged the eventual development of independent states with one powerful city centre controlling a surrounding territory. Communications in Etruscan times were more difficult than they are today not only because the roads were fewer and poorer but also because of the much heavier forest cover. Some of the forests, such as the Ciminian forest north of Sutri, are now mere relics of the impenetrable barriers they formed in antiquity.

Such was the general character of the country in which Etruscan civilization developed. The most vital element in that development, as ancient writers so clearly recognized, was the fact that this country was the most richly endowed by nature in the whole of the Mediterranean world. The fertility of the land was proverbial, and justly so. The valleys of the north-east, the fields around Fiesole and Arretium, produced excellent grain; Pliny the Elder thought the wheat of Clusium the best in the world. In the south, too, though husbandry was a harder task, the soil was rich in potash and soda of volcanic origin. Spring-sown flax was one of the chief crops of Tarquinia from which her famous linen was produced. Of vineyards, the best, then as now, were in the area of modern Tuscany, but the southern zone also produced highly respectable wines. The olive was apparently a late-comer, and much less extensively grown than it is today; a large amount of oil was always imported – for oil the Etruscans had a Greek word, *eleiva*, indicating their source of supply – and less widely used than in Greece.

From its rich forests, Etruria provided one of the chief Mediterranean sources of timber. Theophrastus records that in their forests of beech the Etruscans could fell single trees large enough to form the keels of their ships. The city of Rusellae exploited the forests of fir in the Umbrian basin, which yielded not only supplies of timber but also of charcoal used in the smelting of metals. The forests of mast-yielding trees – beech, oak, and chestnut – provided the fodder for rearing pigs. The forest cover and the relatively high relief produced a more ample rainfall on the western side of the Apennines (36–50 inches per annum) and created conditions suitable for the rearing of cattle and horses; although stock-raising on a large scale was a later phenomenon, there is no doubt that meat was far less a luxury in Etruria than in the more southerly parts of Italy and the Mediterranean in general. Cows and oxen were reared, and horses too, though they remained the luxury of the rich; oxen were used in agriculture in preference to the expensive horse, and mules and oxen were the chief draught animals. The valleys of the Arno and the Chiana had excellent meadows and wet pasture, with good cattle and sheep and famous cheese. In the forests and hills wild boar and deer were hunted, and hunting was always a favourite sport; coastal fishing was widely practised and some of the inland lakes were well stocked with freshwater fish.

If the basis of Etruria's internal economy remained agricultural, a vital reason for her prosperity was the wealth of metal ores, found mainly in the western, coastal areas of the country. The whole Maremma zone, including the modern provinces of Pisa, Livorno, Siena and Grosseto – the so-called Catena Metallifera – is rich in mineral resources of all kinds. Just offshore lies the island of Elba with its wealth of iron ores. The region of Campiglia not far from Populonia has copper, iron, tin and lead; there are rich mines in the areas of Massa Marittima, of Volterra, of Follonica, and Monte Amiata. Farther south, the region of La Tolfa behind Caere has iron, copper and argentiferous lead. Most of the mines were exploited from an early period and were one of the principal reasons why Greek traders and others were attracted to the country. The metals had an easy outlet through the harbours of the coastal cities. Populonia, the only Etruscan city founded on the coast, guarded a good natural harbour and dealt with a large part of the copper trade; later it handled the iron ore imported from Elba.

The Etruscans, if nothing else, were successful in exploiting the rich resources of their country. They won a reputation for sound agricultural economy and the careful husbandry that was needed to maintain the fertility of the inland valleys. They used efficient agricultural tools of iron and understood some of the principles of crop rotation. In the southern volcanic zone they may have practised a special type of forestry which involved rotation between cereals and trees and shrubs suitable for charcoal, the rotation being carried out in carefully walled plots. Deforestation, which they practised

13

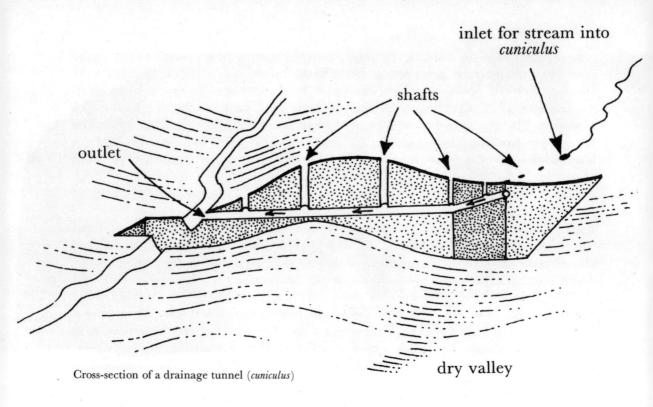

inlet for stream into
cuniculus

shafts

outlet

dry valley

Cross-section of a drainage tunnel (*cuniculus*)

as ruthlessly as other ancient Mediterranean peoples, was not yet beginning to show its disastrous effects of denuding the country of soil, but the Etruscans have a reputation, largely deserved, for success in the constant battle against erosion, silting and flooding. In the volcanic belt of southern Etruria underground tunnels cut in the rock, the so-called *cuniculi*, abound; their purpose was to act as outlets carrying streams from one valley to another, or as drainage channels. One group of these *cuniculi*, over 14 miles in length, centres round the ancient city of Veii and is probably to be associated with the city in its heyday. The Ponte Sodo tunnel which carries the Valchetta stream through a rocky headland near Veii probably dates from before the fifth century. The draining of the marshy forum area in Rome is traditionally attributed to the Etruscan kings, and some of the oldest stretches of the Cloaca Maxima have the corbelled vaulting which is characteristic of early Etruscan tombs. The draining of the fertile Po valley is usually credited to the Etruscan colonists who occupied it in the sixth century, and, if it is doubtful whether the Etruscans were able to arrest the development of marshland in the coastal Maremma, they must take some credit for the fact that the Val di Chiana, a chronic swamp from A.D. 1200 to 1700, was one of the most fertile parts of their country.

Their metallurgy was at least moderately efficient, and if they did not succeed in extracting the maximum of metal from their ores, it must be remembered that these ores were abundant. Many remains of their mines can still be seen in the region of Campiglia near Populonia. In the zone of Val Fucinaia there are open-cast mines, shafts and galleries going back to the eighth century B.C. and examples of their smelting furnaces have been found. They took steps to improve the internal and external communications on which their trade and industry so much depended. The natural lines of communi-

Remains of a smelting furnace from Val Fucinaia

cation, often very difficult, were improved by some considerable works of engineering, like the broad and deep cuttings of the road that links Tarquinia and Sutri with the Faliscan country. In the tufa region it is possible to see many such deep cuttings in the rock scored by wheel-ruts; a number of them must go back to early times. In the Tarquinian territory Bieda seems to have been the centre of a fairly elaborate road system and the lines of several other Etruscan roads, rock-cut and unpaved, are known; among them is the road, perhaps a kind of sacred way, between Caere and Pyrgi, its port. Some stretches of Etruscan road were later incorporated in the famous Roman roads which ran through Etruria to the north. The chief forms of transport were mules and other pack animals, but covered waggons and farm carts could have been seen passing between towns and villages; in winter many of these roads must have been flooded, but efforts were made to make them viable by cutting drainage channels along their line.

Chapter Two

ORIGINS

Only the Garden of Eden may be said to have had an indigenous population, and, naturally, we want to know who the Etruscans were and where they came from. These are questions which used to be in the forefront but are now receding into the background of Etruscan studies. In the modern world a man is more readily judged for what he is than for his ancestry, and an ancient people for their historical relationships rather than their origins. So it is with the Etruscans. We do know something of their racial characteristics, for what that may be worth. They were long-headed and rather short in the mass and they tended to aspirate. They had long faces and narrow noses; the average height of the men was 5 feet 4½ inches and of the women 5 feet 1 inch. They acquired a reputation for running to fat. We may, some day, know their predominant genes, but no one would make confident assertions about their racial type.

There is a legend that the Etruscans were immigrants from Lydia in northern Asia Minor. In the days of a certain King Atys, so the story goes, there was a great and persistent famine in the land of the Lydians and, when all else failed, the final solution was taken to divide the nation and make the two halves draw lots, one to stay and the other to leave the land. Tyrrhenus, the king's son, led the emigrating group which went down to Smyrna, built ships and sailed away, to arrive eventually in the land of Umbria where they settled. They gave up calling themselves Lydians and took the name Tyrrhenians, the Greek name for the Etruscans, from their leader. In itself, this is hardly a likely tale, and it gains little from being widely accepted in antiquity and recounted in its canonical form by the great Greek historian, Herodotus. Coolly assessing it, one would say that it goes back to a Greek source not earlier than the sixth century B.C., which was eagerly swallowed by the philhellene Etruscans of the day. Few people would accept it as it stands, but the tale still conditions, indeed it dominates, all the argument that has raged so long over the Etruscans, by creating a conviction that the Etruscans as we know them must have come from somewhere and that all we need to know is where that somewhere was. Know it, and we will know why they spoke a language different from their neighbours, why their religion had certain distinctive elements; we will understand everything, in fact, that they did not obviously draw from some other known source. It is, of course, an utterly wrong approach, fortunately now in its dying gasp; yet as recently as 1958 the interesting conference held at the C.I.B.A. Foundation in London to discuss the contribution that human genetics could make to the study of the Etruscans conceived the problem essentially in these terms. And if the idea of a mass migration has few adherents nowadays there is still a variant suggesting that an élite element, preferably from the east, arrived to give the vital spark – a more insidious doctrine, hard to prove or disprove, which might very well be true.

If we abandon the ancient story and all it implies we are left with the evidence of archaeology for what it will tell us about the prehistoric development of human occupation in the land of the Etruscans. But the limitations of archaeology in this context must be recognized. What we are interested in is the development of an historical civilization, and the further we look back into prehistory the more out of touch we become with the specific character of what we seek to explain. It will certainly be interesting, and it may be significant, to establish, as far as archaeology can, the movement of people within this area since remotest prehistory, but we have no reason to expect that it will provide a total explanation of the Etruscans. It may not even be possible to solve any of the major problems of Etruscan life. The Etruscans of historical times spoke a language which is different from that of their immediate neighbours and most probably belongs to a different linguistic group; we would like to know when the inhabitants of the area began to speak it and what its affinities are, and we would hope to be able to relate it in some way to the prehistory of the area. But the records of the Etruscan language begin in the seventh century B.C. when it was first written down, and we must not expect to be able to establish when it arrived because, like the Etruscans, it did not necessarily "arrive" but may itself be the result of a long and complex development.

The prehistoric background of any area is always relevant to the people who occupied it in historical times. Etruria is well-favoured for prehistoric settlement from the earliest times. There are traces of the remote palaeolithic hunters, but the first really significant influx of people took place after 5000 B.C. when the first farmers reached the Italian peninsula. They came, it would seem, from the opposite side of the Adriatic, if one may judge from the fact that it was in Italy east of the Apennines that they settled most intensively. These neolithic farmers were, apparently, of what is called typically Mediterranean stock; short, slight and long-headed. They practised a settled agriculture, lived in villages and made respectable pottery. They moved westwards to reach the fertile valleys of Tuscany by 3500 B.C., but many probably came from north and south for this was a period of great movement of population. The use of copper became known in Italy about 2000 B.C. Evidence suggests that the introduction of new metallurgical techniques was accompanied by a fairly large-scale immigration of people of a different physical type, predominantly round-headed; and there is little doubt that it was the rich metal resources of Tuscany that attracted them. Their culture, the so-called Rinaldone, flourished especially in Tuscany, Umbria, and Latium, and certainly exploited the local copper ores. We know these people, as we know so many prehistoric people, only from their tombs, but they seem to have been warriors, in an age of warfare and upheaval. In their burial customs there is much, but most of it, no doubt, fortuitous, to compare with the Etruscans of history. They were stock-breeders rather than agriculturalists and exploited the richer pastures of the western Apennine slopes.

Italy has no colourful Bronze Age to match the splendours of the Aegean world, but the introduction of the new metal, an alloy of copper and tin, was clearly another vital stage in the development of the Italian people. It began perhaps about the time of the Shaft Graves of Mycenae (1650–1500 B.C.). Tuscany and its mines were, no doubt, the centre of its growth, but there is no clear sign of any influx of new population when it began. Metal technology at first was poor but improved rapidly; by the late Bronze

Age, about 1400 B.C., there had developed a culture, the so-called Apennine culture, which brought something like unity to a large part of the country. Its economic basis, apart from the metal industry, was still successful stock-breeding in the Apennine valleys where sheep, goats, cows and pigs were bred but, as yet, no horses. The handsome burnished pottery of the Apennine people shows decorative patterns that seem to be relevant to the styles of Etruria, especially the geometric patterns filled with white inlay. Some tantalizing remains of Apennine religious sites are known; some of their hilltop sanctuaries probably remained places of veneration into historical times.

By now there were close trading links between Italy in the south and the rich Aegean world, both by way of the Adriatic and along the Tyrrhenian; and from 1400 there must have been regular contact with the cities of the Mycenaean world and a good deal of Mycenaean settlement in the extreme south. Recently Mycenaean pottery has been found in central Italy, and local pottery styles may have been influenced by it. In the last years of the Italian Bronze Age when the southern contacts broke down there was no obvious decline but a re-orientation of trade towards the north which brought greater prosperity to Tuscany and increasing northern imports, especially amber from the Baltic by way of the Po valley. Closer links were now forged with the settlers in the Po valley, the people of the Terremare, who at the beginning of the Bronze Age had introduced the rite of urned cremation and who had long practised a skilled bronze craft. Mingling with Apennine settlers from the south, the Terremare people looked for markets and outlets to the north and a new and flourishing phase of the metal industry came into being. One result of this intercourse was the spread of the burial rite of urned cremation, with the burials grouped into characteristic urnfields. There is evidence, too, of considerable changes in the way of life, in manners of dress and personal ornament with the use of the metal fibula or safety pin becoming much more common. These changes were taking place around the tenth century, just before the use of iron made its first appearance in Italy.

The advantages of iron over bronze are well-known; it is more durable and harder. But it is more difficult to work and to find. The use of iron, in very small quantities at first, appears to begin in Italy in the ninth century B.C. and with it we are on the fringes of history and, almost, face to face with the Etruscans. The early Iron Age culture of Etruria still goes by the name Villanovan which it takes from the village of Villanova near Bologna where tombs were excavated and first studied over 100 years ago. The culture is common to Etruria and a large part of the Po valley and is unquestionably the most advanced of the Iron Age cultures of Italy. Our knowledge of its early phases and development is almost entirely derived from tombs, although we are beginning to know more about the settlement sites, especially in Etruria. The cemeteries, which have been fairly extensively explored, were grouped on the slopes of the hills surrounding the settlements. These settlements practised a village economy which was basically agricultural but they also developed a flourishing metal industry, exploiting the resources of the country. The result was a period of greater material prosperity and of great increase in population. The sites of the Villanovan villages in the Etruscan homeland coincide with those which later became Etruscan cities and settlements; all the great Etruscan cities, Veii, Tarquinia, Vulci and the rest, have a Villanovan background.

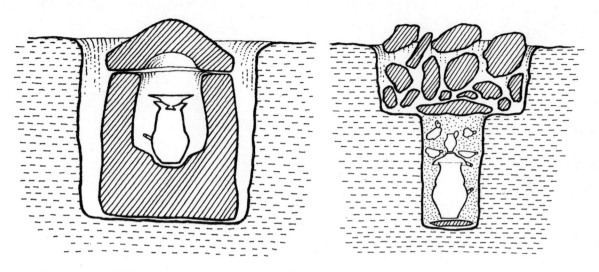

Cross-section of Villanovan cremation burials at Caere

In the cemeteries the prevailing burial rite is cremation with burnt bones placed in a pot made of black earthenware and of a characteristic biconical shape which is set in a cylindrical hole cut in rock or soil. The hole may have a cover of some sort and may be lined with slabs of stone; variations from place to place are minor and generally unimportant. The pot itself may have one handle or two handles, of which one is deliberately broken off, at its widest point, and it may be covered with a shallow cup or with a clay helmet. Small objects, the possessions of the dead, are placed inside the pot or outside it in the hole. The individual burials are closely grouped together in burial grounds which are generally known as urnfields. Although iron is a rarity in the early Villanovan graves, there is no doubt that a major cultural change took place at the time when these urnfields first appear, and it is a matter of vital importance to establish its causes. Because the earliest European urnfields lie across the Alps in Hungary it is tempting to think of some northern invasion on a fairly massive scale, especially since some of the equipment of the dead appears to have northern affinities. On the other hand, the type of cinerary urn which characterizes the Villanovan burials seems to be a local form developed from earlier Apennine shapes, and many of the incised geometric decorative patterns are locally inspired. Other objects, especially the fibulae, which are found in large quantities in the burials, are locally developed, though related to types elsewhere.

The earliest phase of the Villanovan in Etruria, now more commonly called Archaic I, may be reckoned from about 850 to 750 B.C. The chronology is quite uncertain, since the graves contain no material that can be precisely dated. This is the pure Villanovan, with cremation the universal rite. The burials are simple, with pottery urns and modest grave-goods; some burials are richer than others, but there is little suggestion of major divisions of wealth or prestige. Male burials often have a helmet serving as the lid of the urn; daggers of bronze, razors and various objects of personal adornment are often found in them. The fibula with a spiral catchplate is a typical form of the period, and there are very few imported objects. Amber, the product of trade with the

19

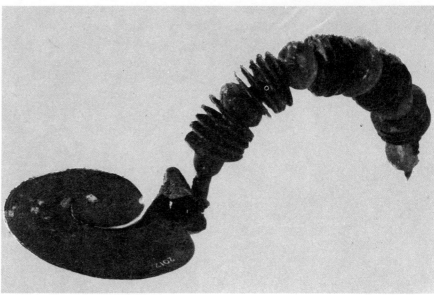

Left. Villanovan cremation urn from Tarquinia with a bronze helmet serving as the lid. *Right*. Bronze fibula with spiral catchplate and amber beads on the bow. Eighth century B.C.

north, is fairly common, but there is nothing obviously from the Mediterranean world. It is now generally agreed that the Villanovan developed earlier in Etruria than in the Bolognese, which would make Etruria the start of a movement which later spread across the Apennine passes into the Po valley, and was based largely on the metal resources of the Etruscan homeland.

By about 750 B.C., therefore, a basically uniform culture, though with certain regional differences, prevailed in Etruria and parts of the Po valley, influenced strongly by northern contacts but arising, it would seem, from a fusion of urnfield elements and the late Apennine culture of the area. Then, in the second half of the eighth century, the picture begins to change, and the Etruscan area begins an independent development which results in the appearance of a distinct Etruscan culture. The uniformity of the Villanovan culture is broken up, and its various centres begin to show regional characteristics; and although these regional differences are known only from burial customs they must reflect major changes in the way of life. This is the period known as Archaic II in Etruria; its limits can only be approximately dated but it is clear that some burials of this period contain imported Greek pottery as early as, if not earlier than, the pottery found in the graves of the earliest Greek colonists at Cumae which is generally believed to have been founded about 750 B.C.

The chief characteristic of the cemeteries of Archaic II is the fact that in most places cremation ceases to be the universal burial rite and in some inhumation appears on a fairly large scale. At Tarquinia, for example, of the 86 burials recorded for the period, 58 are inhumations. At Vetulonia, in the north, the proportion is very much smaller and at inland Clusium (Chiusi) the impact of inhumation is hardly felt at all. The change in burial rite need not, in itself, be of great historical significance, but it is certainly contemporary with, and perhaps symptomatic of, major changes in social conditions. The earliest inhumations are not much richer than the pits of Archaic I, but as the period progresses there are signs of a very general increase in wealth with decorated bronze cinerary urns and richer and more varied bronze jewellery. At Tarquinia the trench graves, and a few more elaborate corridor tombs, are richly equipped. The men's tombs contain more varied armour – shoulder-pieces, round shields of hammered bronze elaborately decorated with repoussé ornament, pectorals, lances with leaf-shaped points. Iron is more common and is used for lance-heads and daggers. At Vetulonia the pits of Archaic I had contained very limited arms and armour – lance-heads, a few iron daggers and swords with bronze sheaths; defensive armour consisted only of helmets. But in the succeeding period the repertoire is vastly increased with more iron lance-heads and other weapons; and there is much more armour including big round shields, greaves, and helmets of different kinds. The grave goods in general show wider contacts and greatly increased prosperity; imported Greek vases, a few eastern imports and, in the late phases of Archaic II, the appearance of precious metals.

More important than the general increase in prosperity is the fact that from about 700 B.C. most of the Etruscan burial grounds have some exceptionally wealthy tombs, or groups of tombs, isolated in some way or by some special treatment from the rest of the burials, and sometimes strikingly different in scale. They reflect quite clearly the rise of a ruling class, the warrior aristocracy which appears to have controlled the fortunes of the Etruscan cities in their earliest days. The Tomb of the Warrior at Tarquinia is a rich sarcophagus burial dated around 700 B.C. and the well-known Bocchoris Tomb is perhaps not much later. At Vetulonia in the early seventh century the burials of prominent families are isolated by rings of stones covered with mounds. At Populonia rectangular chamber-tombs with circular vaults are buried under tumuli, and in the fully developed types the tumulus is raised on a cylindrical drum. At Clusium the so-called *ziro* tombs, cremation burials in large pots, are found in well-defined groups and contain rich bronze objects and some imitation Greek pottery. It is interesting to contrast the development in Etruria with that of the Villanovan in the area around Bologna. In the earliest period, as in Etruria, the tombs are very uniform in their contents; in the seventh century, although there is a general increase in wealth, there is little evidence for special areas of burial or richer tombs of a dominating class. The presence of horse-bits in some of the tombs may perhaps suggest the rise of a horse-owning aristocracy but the contrast with the rich burials of Etruria remains a very striking one.

The period known as Archaic III begins in Etruria about 675 B.C. It varies in detail from place to place but its general character is clear. It is an age of enhanced prosperity with imports flooding in from Greece and from the eastern Mediterranean. The burials of the wealthy are accompanied by incredible riches and stand in massive isolation. In the south the zone of great tumuli covering rock-cut or built chambers includes Caere, Veii and Tarquinia. The Regolini-Galassi tomb at Caere is one of the few that has been discovered intact; it was built in a Villanovan burial ground, the Sorbo cemetery, which lies immediately south of the city. The tomb, partly cut in the rock and partly constructed of stones bedded horizontally and overlapping one another to form a kind of vault, consisted of a long open corridor leading into a narrow rect-

angular chamber. Two niches were cut in the walls of the corridor which was subsequently roofed over to create a further burial chamber. There were three burials, the first a cremation of a man in the right-hand niche, the second an inhumation of a woman in the main chamber, and finally the burial of a man in the outer chamber with his grave goods filling the left niche as well. The exceptional preservation of these burials is explained by the fact that the tumulus was raised and extended to cover five later tombs around it; some of the burials in the surrounding tombs are as late as the fifth century B.C. The cremation in the right-hand niche of the original tomb contained the ashes of a man in a large urn surmounted by the figure of a horseman; buried with this warrior aristocrat were his bronze chariot and his weapons of war. In the main chamber a woman was buried, laid on her funeral bed clad in rich clothes and jewellery; surrounding her were possessions of gold and silver and nearby a throne. Last to be buried was the occupant of the outer chamber. He lay on a bronze bed fully armed; near him was a four-wheeled vehicle and in the right niche his chariot and many precious objects.

There were once many tombs of equal splendour in southern Etruria. The Avvolta Tumulus at Tarquinia, discovered in 1823, was another multi-chambered tomb of exceptional size and fine construction; its rich grave goods have been dispersed but it is known that the man buried in it wore a gold crown. Perhaps he was one of the early rulers of the place. There were princely burials of the same kind at Veii, among them the Vaccareccia Tumulus and the Chigi Tomb. In the north the types of tombs are different. The zone of Circle Tombs includes Vetulonia and Marsiliana d'Albegna. At Vetulonia, in the period approximately contemporary with the tumuli of the south, the burials are grouped in stone circles varying from approximately 18 to 25 yards in diameter, and are very rich in precious metals and foreign imports. The finest of the Circle Tombs is the Tomba del Duce, the burial of a man of great importance, containing no less than five separate deposits, one a chariot burial. In the vast burial ground of the Banditella at Marsiliana there are circle tombs enclosing one or more inhumation burials, rich in gold, silver, ivory and bronze. Here again the isolation of the tomb as a monumental entity corresponds with the growth of luxury. The Tumulus of the Chariots in the cemetery of Podere di S. Cerbone at Populonia was one of the richest graves of the period, but very little of its wealth in gold and ivory has survived; in the rooms flanking the entrance to the tomb were two chariots with their wheels and bodies of oak covered with bronze inlaid with iron.

The evidence of burial customs reflects the transformation of the Villanovan Iron Age in the late eighth and seventh centuries. The most obvious feature is the creation of a dominating upper class which became the historical aristocracy of Etruria. Great wealth is shown by the mass of foreign imports from Greece and the East, and by a flourishing local production of luxury goods. Prosperity was mainly due to the successful exploitation of the mineral resources of the country which drew the Greeks, through their Italian colonies, and other oriental traders into contact with Etruria and provided vital stimuli for the development of Etruscan civilization. Much of what we think of as typically Etruscan came from these sources. By the middle of the seventh century foreign contacts had given the Etruscans an alphabet, inspired their art, and deeply influenced their way of life. It seems clear that during this period of foreign influences

View of the main chamber of the Regolini-Galassi Tomb, Caere

Reconstructed chariot of wood and bronze from the Regolini-Galassi Tomb

Greeks and orientals came and stayed, some permanently, in Etruria, but there is no reason to suppose that there was a new immigration of a large ethnic group. The archaeological evidence, indeed, suggests that there was not. At Clusium there is little doubt that the people who were buried in the rich *ziro* burials were the successors of their Villanovan forebears, made richer by trade and commerce. In the south the contrast between the massive built tombs and the modest Villanovan cremation pits might seem, at first sight, to imply a distinction between native and foreigner, but, in fact, the big tombs indicate very strong cultural contacts with the preceding phases of the Etruscan Iron Age. At Tarquinia the development from the first inhumation trenches to the late chamber tombs is direct and clear, and the picture is very much the same at Veii where the closely-packed shafts with cremation burials were followed by trench

Above right. Gold pectoral with repoussé decoration from the Regolini-Galassi Tomb. *Right*. Circle tomb in the S. Cerbone cemetery at Populonia

graves to which lateral extensions were added for more grave furniture and then large recesses. The fully-fledged chamber tomb is merely the final development. It is a progressive development rather than a violent change which is shown in the burial customs of such places as Vetulonia and Populonia. The same is true of the accompanying armour, ritual vessels, and objets d'art. And there is certainly no archaeological evidence for the kind of colonization that the Greeks undertook in southern Italy and Sicily, which produces a clear-cut distinction between native and foreign graves.

We cannot find archaeological evidence for any single immigration, to explain in comparatively simple terms the traditions and way of life of the historical Etruscans. Archaeology provides no simple answer; indeed, it makes quite clear the fact that no simple answer is possible. Our picture of the prehistoric development of Etruria shows an area which, because of its wealth in natural resources, had many times been the centre of creative cultural changes. The rise of the Rinaldone culture in the Copper Age, the prosperity of the region in the late Bronze Age, and the establishment of the historical pattern of settlement in the flourishing Iron Age are all phases vital to the understanding of the historical Etruscans. Certainly the archaeological picture, which depends on the as yet limited results of excavation, is oversimplified. We cannot tell what vital contacts with the outside world may have taken place but have left no evidence for archaeology; at any time in this long period, new people, who might explain some element of the historical civilization of the Etruscans, may have appeared. No part of the ancient world, after all, is so thickly sown with recollections of Odysseus, the wanderer who symbolizes, it seems, the migratory movements of Aegean peoples in the late Bronze Age. In one account he is slain in Tyrrhenia, and, says Hesiod, his descendants rule over all the high-famed Tyrrhenians. Such persistent traditions may well have a basis in fact, but archaeology so far has not revealed it.

The problem of the origins of the Etruscan language illustrates most clearly the limitations of the archaeological evidence in explaining the facts of history. We know that by the middle of the seventh century B.C. some Etruscans were literate; the earliest inscriptions are found on pottery from the rich tombs of the period. The structure of the language of the inscriptions is different from those of the neighbours of the Etruscans, most of whom spoke dialects which have in common a basic system of sounds, inflections and word-formation which is called Indo-European. Etruscan, though influenced by these dialects, does not seem to belong to the same group. The three main non-Indo-European languages of Italy are Etruscan, Ligurian and Raetic; the Indo-European languages fall into three main groups – Italic, including Picene and Iapygian, Osco-Umbrian in the centre, and Latin. Etruscan has been classified in a general sense as a Mediterranean language and it has obvious affinities with some other Mediterranean dialects including, most closely, the dialect spoken in historical times on the island of Lemnos. Connections with the languages of western Asia Minor, among them Lydian and Lycian, exist, but are less strong. The problem of deciding when and how the language was introduced in Etruria is a vital one. It has been argued that the three main groups of Indo-European dialects in Italy represent successive waves of Indo-European influence, and as the non-Indo-European languages occupy, generally speaking, the western side of the peninsula it may be supposed that these waves moved from east to west, with Latin perhaps as the earliest to arrive. Etruscan would then be a survivor in the extreme west of a pre-Indo-European or Mediterranean language. But if this picture of the process is correct, archaeology offers little to confirm it; it gives us little clue to when the first Indo-European speakers arrived, whether in the Copper Age or in the Bronze, though it suggests that they must have arrived long before the introduction of iron, as we know they did in Greece. The very general correspondence between the cremating Iron Age cultures and the areas of non-Indo-European speech and between the inhuming cultures and the Indo-European, is too vague to be the basis of a serious hypothesis.

We are nearer to the truth, it seems, if we reject the simple, and oversimplified, opposition between Indo-European and non-Indo-European. The "Mediterranean" theory, once widely held in Italy, is now being modified; Etruscan is not simply a "Mediterranean" language but has a Mediterranean substratum contributing important elements to its formation. The Etruscan language itself is the result of a long process of formation, so that Dionysius of Halicarnassus was probably right when he said that the Etruscans spoke a language unlike that of any other people. As a result of many changes and influences the Etruscan language took its final shape in Italy. In any case, there is no reason to think that the language was introduced by a group of invaders from the eastern Mediterranean during the Iron Age. This view of the language coincides with the general position adopted in this book about "the origins of the Etruscans"; that their whole culture is the result of a long process of change with certain vital foreign stimuli on the fringe of history, and it is a view that is amply confirmed by what we know of the historical composition of the Etruscan people. An Etruscan may bear a Latin, or an Umbrian, or an Illyrian name; it can happen, and indeed frequently does, that his *praenomen*, *nomen*, and *cognomen* derive from different languages. He can bear an Osco-Umbrian name like Herinas or Pumpus, a Greek name like Hipucrates, or a name drawn from widely different parts of Italy: Latinies, Kalaprenas, Venetes, Sentinates. There can hardly be any simple answer to the question: who were the Etruscans?

Chapter Three

STATES

The process which we may call the final "Etruscanization" of Etruria is essentially that of the founding of cities. Most of the sites which later became Etruscan cities had been occupied since early Villanovan times by people who practised a village economy; the sites they chose were generally level heights or plateaus surrounded by valleys and ravines, and if possible with a specially well-protected height which could serve as an acropolis in time of trouble. Veii, Caere and Tarquinia are typical. The picture that emerges from those places that have been or are being excavated is one of groups of villages occupying most of the plateau, perhaps with a single system of defence.

Then, at different times and no doubt in different ways, these village communities were transformed into single urban nuclei. We do not know precisely when or how it happened; indeed, it was probably a gradual process. We have no foundation dates for Etruscan cities as we have for the Greek colonies in southern Italy. In some of the south Etruscan cities the evidence suggests that several small settlements were combined in the process; at Vetulonia it looks as if two rather large Villanovan communities were formed into a single city. Some of the cities were probably late developers; Vulci, for example, was an important Villanovan place, but the process of urbanization may not have taken place until the early sixth century. But, whenever it happened, the process seems to be basically the same everywhere; the foundation of the cities arises out of the social and topographical framework of the Iron Age settlements.

The source of the formative urge seems clear enough. From the earlier eighth century onwards the Greeks had been in close contact with Etruria which provided the raw materials they needed and excellent markets for their own products. The spread of ideas from Greece and the eastern Mediterranean, reflected in the ever increasing importation of foreign objects, would account for the urbanization of the Etruscan area. If so, it is arguable that the process began in the coastal areas which were the main avenues by which foreign contacts penetrated. The settlements nearest the coast quickly established harbours to receive foreign traders, and their development may be expected to have been the most rapid. The inland cities may have developed as Etruscan centres appreciably later than their counterparts near the coast. We can say very little about the events which accompanied the founding of cities. Some scholars have thought, and still think, that the establishment of Etruscan rule in Italy was the result of a great warlike enterprise, the concerted effort of a minority group made possible by superior organization and military strength. This view stems from the conception of the Etruscans as an invading minority, imposing its power by right of conquest on an alien people, a conception which, at least, seems to have no archaeological foundation. It was certainly a warlike age, but the process of urbanization which implies so complete an integration of the existing society groups may still have been a largely peaceful one.

Our general impression of seventh-century Etruria is of a large number of prosperous and probably independent communities with limited territories, many of which peter out in the sixth century or lose their independence to a comparatively small number of more powerful cities; the latter extend their territories to make the typical Etruscan city-state of historical times – a large urban nucleus controlling an area of land including smaller townships, villages and defensive sites. Colonization from the main centres, military conquest of the less powerful, and peaceful expansion are some of the factors by which the power of the chief cities grew. History is almost silent on what must have been one of the most colourful periods of Etruscan history; very soon the cities came into the control of powerful rulers of whose personalities and deeds we know nothing. There is scarcely a legend about them; just a few names in Latinized forms, like Mezentius of Caere in Virgil's *Aeneid* who symbolizes the Etruscan oppression of the Latins, and Propertius, an early king of Veii. Daniel's Servius preserves an interesting tradition about the character of early Etruscan expansion with his story of the colonization of Capena, a town within the Faliscan territory. The Faliscans spoke a Latin dialect and were never fully Etruscanized, but they came under strong Etruscan influence from an early period, and Falerii and Capena were, in effect, Etruscan cities. Servius says that the colonization of Capena was carried out by a band of young men from Veii in accordance with the strange rite known as the "Sacred Spring" whereby a community offered to its gods the total material product for one year, including the children born. The children in this case were not sacrificed but when they reached manhood were driven beyond the frontiers of the state and ordered by Propertius, the king, to found the new colony. The account is plausible as an event in the second-stage expansion of the Etruscan cities into territories which, although conquered by Etruscan force of arms, did not give up their old way of life and preserved their old language and customs. It is a different pattern from Etruria proper where a virtually homogeneous culture prevailed and a single language predominated.

There is still much to be learnt about the Etruscan cities and about the character and extent of their territories. No city has yet been thoroughly explored, and the sites of many have not yet been identified. Caletra in the Albegna valley has disappeared and there is still controversy about the site of ancient Volsinii. Thorough survey of the territories of the city-states is only just beginning and we do not know the precise boundaries between one state and another. In the map on page 30 the boundaries of the chief city-states are tentatively marked together with the chief Etruscan sites at present known. The names of cities and towns are mostly given in the Latinized forms that are generally used, but the Etruscan versions of most are known. Volterra was *Velathri*, Populonia *Pupluna*, Tarquinia probably *Tarchuna*, and Caere was called *Cisra*, although it also had a Greek name, *Agylla*. Some recorded place-names, for example *Thezi*, which appears on coins, have not been identified, and we do not know the ancient names for a number of obviously important sites.

A few miles north of Rome, at the confluence of two branches of the Cremera river, stood the city of Veii; it occupied a level plateau with a spur of higher ground, the Piazza d'Armi, which served as its acropolis. The territory of the state is believed to

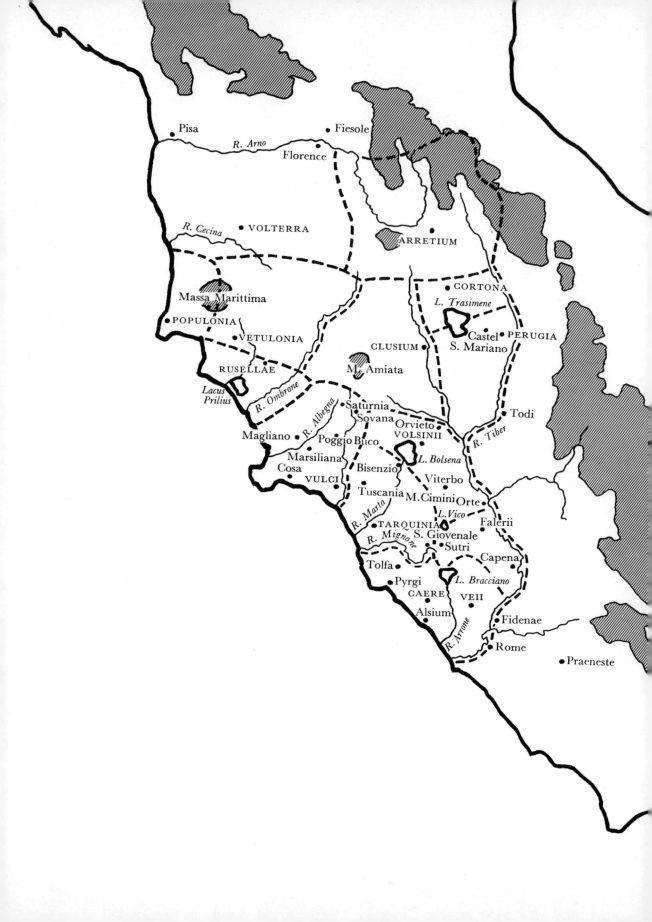

Pisa

Fiesole

R. Arno

Florence

R. Cecina • VOLTERRA

ARRETIUM

Massa Marittima

• CORTONA

L. Trasimene

• POPULONIA

• VETULONIA

CLUSIUM

Castel
S. Mariano • PERUGIA

RUSELLAE

M. Amiata

Todi

*Lacus
Prilius*

R. Ombrone

Saturnia

Orvieto
Sovana VOLSINII

R. Tiber

Magliano *R. Albegna*

Poggio Buco

L. Bolsena

Marsiliana

Bisenzio Viterbo

Cosa VULCI

Tuscania M. Cimini Orte

R. Marta

L. Vico Falerii

R. Mignone TARQUINIA
S. Giovenale

Tolfa Sutri

Capena

Pyrgi *L. Bracciano*

CAERE VEII

Alsium *R. Arrone* Fidenae

Rome

• Praeneste

Aerial view of Veii; the Piazza d'Armi, the acropolis of the city, lies at the southern end of the promontory (right hand side of picture)

have reached to the sea on the west, taking in a narrow strip of land between the Tiber and the south Arrone which formed its frontier with Caere; eastwards and to the north it took in a belt of country between Lago di Vico and Bracciano, extending perhaps as far north as Sutri. Veii had close contacts with the whole Faliscan territory, and traditionally, as we have seen, Capena was her colony. The natural frontier between Veii and the Faliscans was the densely wooded Monti Sabatini. Fidenae in the territory of Capena was Veii's bridgehead on the Tiber, linking her by way of Palestrina with the south.

The territory of Caere bounded Veii on the north-west. The city was some four miles from the sea, situated on a flat-topped ridge of tufa between deep gorges; it lay about twenty miles north of Rome on the edge of the hills and looking over the coastal plains towards the sea. The Mignone river and the Tolfa mountains formed its northern frontier and its hinterland stretched to Lago di Bracciano. In its long stretch of coast there were several harbours including Alsium near Palo, Punicum (S. Marinella) and Pyrgi (S. Severa), its chief port. The city itself was about 375 acres in extent and the whole of its territory about 500 square miles, if we assume that it stretched south to a point between Fregenae and the mouth of the Tiber, leaving a narrow corridor of access to the sea for its neighbour, Veii. A number of sites within Caere's territory are known. The wooded volcanic mountains of the Tolfa region are rich in metals and were densely occupied from the seventh century; a number of roads linked the area with the capital. The chief port of Pyrgi with its sanctuaries is now in process of excavation, though the coastal currents have largely eaten away the harbour itself. Castellina was Caere's frontier town on the north. It stood above the wooded valley of the Mignone, in a strong position that commanded the harbour at the mouth of the river and the road giving access to the interior with its woods of oak and chestnut and rich mineral deposits. It was clearly a prosperous place, fortified as a frontier town in the late sixth century.

Tarquinia extended from the Mignone to the Arrone and inland to the region between Bolsena and Bracciano; the wooded hills of the Ciminian mountains formed its boundary with the Faliscans. Its territory, to judge from the large number of smaller settlements, was clearly one of the most populous in the whole of Etruria. Graviscae and Martanum were two of its harbours; Tuscania and Visentium on Lake Bolsena were prosperous settlements within its territory which also included Bieda, Norchia and Castel d'Asso in the district of Viterbo, famous for their rock-cut tombs. S. Giovenale, now in process of excavation, was another prosperous town which in later times may have become a defensive outpost. The site of Tarquinia itself is a plateau known as La Città, some five miles from the sea; it covered an area not much smaller than that of Caere, its neighbour.

Vulci, Tarquinia's neighbour to the north, had at the height of its power the largest territory in southern Etruria, reaching along the coast from the Uccellina hills to the Arrone and inland comprising the valleys of the Albegna and the Fiora. It was bounded on the north by Rusellae and on the east by Clusium and Volsinii. The city is some eight miles from the sea on a low plateau on the right bank of the Fiora river now known as the Pian di Voce, about the same size as Caere. Only one side of the plateau was strongly defended by nature. It was announced in 1955 that the site, which had long been subjected to notorious clandestine excavation, was to be systematically explored. In Vulci's territory there were numerous smaller towns and villages, among them Sovana, Heba, Talamone, Pitigliano, and Poggio Buco. The last named, in the Fiora valley, was a town of about two miles circuit which flourished in the sixth and seventh centuries but later went into decline. Pitigliano disappeared at the end of the sixth century. Later Saturnia seems to have been the chief town of the Albegna valley, superseding several other settlements which may once have depended on Vetulonia; something of the layout and of the lines of communication from this important centre are known. Cosa, placed on a hill above an estuary which brought ships within a few miles of the city was Vulci's chief port; the valleys of the Albegna and the Fiora were the basis of the city's inland communications.

Volsinii, on the edge of the fertile volcanic zone, was Vulci's eastern neighbour. Its territory reached eastwards to the Tiber and it had frontiers with Clusium on the north and Tarquinia on the south-west. The site of the city is still not certainly identified. Recently it has been argued that it stood on a hill known as Poggio Mozzetta, about a mile or so north of Bolsena. The Mozzetta is an exceptionally strong natural position with a ravine on the north side and was later fortified by formidable walls. Orvieto, the other contender, stands on a great bastion of tufa dominating the middle Tiber valley and, if it was not Volsinii, it was obviously an exceptionally important city in its

Plate 1. Clay cremation urn in the shape of a wattle-and-daub hut. Eighth century B.C. (Villa Giulia, Rome)

territory. It may have been Salpinum which Livy mentions as independent in a period when some of the big city-states had been broken up. Ferentinum, Polimartium and Horte were towns in Volsinii's territory.

North of the Albegna the divisions of the territories of the various states are less clearly defined. The site of Vetulonia has been identified with fair certainty as the plateau known as Colonna di Buriano in the province of Grosseto, about 10 miles from the sea. In its most flourishing period it probably had an extensive territory including large parts of the Albegna valley, where Marsiliana, which has provided some of the most spectacular discoveries for the early period of Etruria, shows close connections with Vetulonia. Vetulonia's wealth and wide connections must have been largely derived from the mines of Massa Marittima. It probably had a number of ports, including the lagoon later known as Lacus Prilius and perhaps Populonia. Vetulonia declined in the sixth century with the rise to power of Vulci in the south and her nearer neighbours Populonia and Rusellae. Marsiliana also faded at the end of the sixth century; its remarkable early prosperity may have been connected with that of Vetulonia. It could have exploited the mines of Amiata and from its commanding position in the middle of the valley controlled a vital route into the interior of the country.

Rusellae rose to prominence as Vetulonia declined. It stood on the summit of a low hill against a higher one on the route linking Vetulonia with Marsiliana. Rusellae was already a place of some importance in the seventh century but its most flourishing period was in the sixth and fifth centuries; in the fifth it was given a circuit of massive polygonal walls and was perhaps one of the earliest Etruscan cities to be defended in this way. Rusellae is at present being systematically excavated and it is to be hoped that the excavations will throw light on the relations of the north-western Etruscan cities. Populonia, on the rugged promontory of Masoncello above a natural harbour, the Golfo di Baratti, is the only major Etruscan city on the sea. It has a Villanovan background and an early "Etruscanization" so the tradition that it was a late foundation may reflect the fact that it was originally dependent on Vetulonia and only came into prominence as an independent city-state in the sixth century. Its early prosperity depended on the copper mines in the area of Campiglia, and from about 400 B.C. it was chiefly an industrial city concerned with the smelting of iron ores shipped from the island of Elba. Vast deposits of iron slag were piled over its early cemeteries of S. Cerbone and Poggio della Porcareccia.

The early history of Volterra in the north remains obscure. Its situation is wonderfully picturesque and immensely powerful, for it stands on a great rock about 30 miles from the sea; its circuit of later walls, $4\frac{1}{2}$ miles in length, make it one of the largest Etruscan places. No rich tombs of the early period have been found so far, and although its neighbourhood has the rich copper mines of the Cecina valley we do not know whether it exploited them. If it had harbours, and should be classed as a coastal state, we do not know where they were; the Cecina valley, however, gave Volterra fairly easy access to the sea. It is sometimes thought that, in fact, Volterra favoured an internal expansion and dominated the valleys that run north towards the Arno, becoming the chief driving force of the later Etruscan expansion into the valley of the Po. It is clear that from the seventh century there were a number of important Etruscan places in the middle valley of the Arno between the river and the Apennines. Fiesole seems to have

Plate 2. Etruscan gold jewellery. Seventh and sixth centuries B.C. (British Museum, London)

35

Rock-cut tombs at Blera, near Viterbo

become the centre of a rich agricultural zone and had close connections with Volterra. The routes to the Po valley via the Ombrone and Reno rivers passed this way and in the course of time Fiesole and Florence grew into respectable towns.

Clusium, most famed of the inland cities of Etruria, included a territory which was perhaps the most fertile in all Etruria. It was slow to develop a full Etruscan culture, preserving the rite of cremation into the sixth century and accepting foreign imports rather later than the coastal cities. Clusium's hill is about 1,300 feet high, surrounded by deep ravines and with the fertile Chiana valley below it; the circuit of its later walls was $1\frac{1}{2}$ miles, its area about 90 acres. The Chiana, at that time a tributary of the Tiber, was apparently navigable as far as the city and reached the Tiber at Orvieto; from there the valley of the river provided communications with the southern states. There were good communications via the Ombrone to the coast at Populonia. Clusium's territory has been estimated at 720 square miles. Its limits extended eastwards to the country beyond Lake Trasimene which was at first sparsely populated with agricultural villages. In the course of the sixth century one or two larger centres developed, among

Part of the walls of Rusellae

them Cortona and Arretium, both of which were to achieve independent fame in later Etruscan history. Cortona had an area of 100 acres and the circuit of its later walls was $1\frac{1}{4}$ miles; it was already a flourishing community in the sixth century. Perugia, on a hill above a valley, lay in Umbrian territory beyond Lake Trasimene with the mountainous heights of the Apennines behind it, and was an important centre of communications. Etruscan finds before the fifth century are sparse, though they include some fine things such as the bronzes from Castel S. Mariano. Perugia always had close connections with Clusium and its development may be the result of Clusium's expansion. Later it became an important and independent place with a largish and fertile territory between the Tiber and Trasimene. The city itself had a circuit of about 2 miles.

The historical tradition tells us that there were twelve chief cities of Etruria in the period of her greatness. This tradition probably goes back to the late sixth century B.C., under the influence of Ionian Greece where there existed a similar league of twelve principal states. But it does seem that this persistent tradition preserves an historical reality, at least, in the sixth and fifth centuries, though it is difficult to name the twelve. The impression one gets is of a large number of prosperous and perhaps independent states in the seventh century which later yielded their independence to the prominent city-states of history; the process was accompanied by a large movement of population into the big cities and coincided with the great period of prosperity of such places as Vulci and Clusium. In the period in which we are interested, one can be sure that Veii, Caere, Tarquinia, Vulci, Clusium and Volsinii were among the most powerful since they figure prominently in historical records. So does Vetulonia, though the evidence suggests that it lost its prominence in the course of the sixth century. Rusellae, Populonia, Arretium, Perugia and Volterra rose to power within the period. This would give us the original twelve states, although Populonia is specifically stated to have been founded later than the twelve. In Roman times the number had been increased to fifteen, reflecting the fact that many smaller communities probably won some form of independence during the struggles for supremacy with Rome.

Chapter Four

HISTORY

We cannot write the history of the Etruscan states. We have no historical writings from Etruscan sources, and when a city such as Veii emerges into history it is seen, however sympathetically, through the eyes of its enemies. That there was a genuine tradition of local history in the chief cities can hardly be doubted and occasionally we get glimpses of it. There were also priestly records, like the records of the *pontifices* in Rome, since divine guidance or divine command must be sought in dramatic moments of history. The paintings of the famous François Tomb at Vulci are obviously based on local Vulcian historical tradition. They recount the exploits of the Vipinas brothers and the hero Macstrna against Tarquin, the king of Rome, who was allied to other southern Etruscan cities. This was in the days of Vulci's great power during the sixth century B.C., and the Vulcian story was apparently followed by that erudite Etruscophile, the Emperor Claudius, if one may judge from a tantalising fragment of his speech on the subject. Semi-legendary "Tuscan Histories" of this kind were the sources from which the learned antiquarians of the late Republic and early Empire – Cato, Varro, Verrius Flaccus and Claudius himself – composed their accounts of Etruscan history. Some genuine Etruscan tradition lies behind the series of commemorative inscriptions dating from the first century A.D. which were found not so long ago on the site of Tarquinia. They praised the deeds of famous Etruscans, from the days of Tarchon, the city's mythical founder, onwards; one inscription refers to a Tarquinian noble, a man of Norchia ($12\frac{1}{2}$ miles east of Tarquinia), who won a victory over the king of Caere, fought against Arretium, and in another campaign captured nine Latin towns. The close connection between military triumph and the rites of the supreme divinity helped to ensure the survival of the records.

To add to this tradition there are just a few contemporary historical documents, like the gold plaques recently discovered at Pyrgi, and the evidence of archaeology which is steadily building up a picture of the commercial and political relations between the various states. But it is well to remember that while archaeology can, and frequently does, confirm an historical or semi-historical tradition, it can hardly ever be a substitute for history, as the raging controversy over the early history of Rome bears clear witness. The most vivid aspects of Etruscan history, accounts of wars and the deeds of famous men, may remain unknown to us for ever.

The rise of the Villanovan civilization in the ninth century was, as we have seen, a vital stage in the development of historical Etruria. There can be no doubt that the Apennine Bronze culture played a large part in the formation of the Villanovans, but outside influences were also very strong. The marked population increase suggests that there was fairly large-scale immigration of individuals or groups of individuals from outside the peninsula and from other parts of Italy. Although we cannot establish the source of all the outside stimuli, we can be sure that there were close connections with south Italy and that there was some immigration from that area; immigrants from the north also came, if one may judge from the archaeological links, which are sometimes quite striking, with the urnfields of continental Europe. The events, therefore, which established the historical pattern of settlement in Etruria must have been accompanied by a fair amount of population change.

After about 800 B.C., progress was very rapid, and by the late seventh century the process of "Etruscanization" had penetrated deep into the interior. Falerii, the modern Civita Castellana, in the territory of the Faliscans who occupied the bend of the Tiber beyond the Monti Sabatini and the Monti Cimini, became a city on the Etruscan pattern with a large Etruscan-speaking element in its population. The Etruscan cities made rapid advances in exploiting their natural resources during the eighth and seventh centuries. Caere was quick to develop the mineral wealth of the Tolfa region, completely changing the character of settlement; many village communities and commercial centres sprang up, linked by roads with the capital of the area. Around 750 B.C. the Etruscans were making their first contacts with the new colonizing enterprise of the Greek city-states. The oldest Greek colony in the west was Cumae on the bay of Naples, founded by Chalcis in Euboea; one of the chief reasons for the choice of the site must have been that it lay in close proximity to the Etruscan sources of metal. Of the earliest relations between Greeks and "Tyrrhenians" history has little to say; the latter made themselves a formidable reputation as pirates, but "Tyrrhenian" was perhaps applied rather generally to the Italic peoples. What evidence we have suggests that trade was carried on successfully between Greeks and Etruscans. The local population was highly receptive to Greek ideas and welcomed at least a limited number of Greek immigrants. In the seventh century a body of Corinthians, led by a nobleman Demaratus, is said to have settled in Tarquinia, and Tarquinia's cemetery has produced an Italo-Geometric pot with a name which implies a man of mixed Greco-Etruscan stock. This early phase of successful intercourse between Greeks and Etruscans was clearly the most vital one in the development of historical Etruscan culture. From Cumae, apparently, the Etruscans got their alphabet and many words in their vocabulary; from the Greeks in general they gained a new stimulus for their art and adopted Greek manners in every branch of life.

Increasing foreign contacts, internal struggles for power and the development of a national consciousness are three main factors of early Etruscan history. How strong their common bond in fact was, is one of the crucial questions for our knowledge of the Etruscan people. The Etruscans certainly acknowledged among themselves common ties of race, language, and culture. In the early period close links were forged between different cities, links which can to some extent be seen in the evidence of archaeology, and although there were obviously regional differences, it is tempting to think of a powerful communal effort as the mainspring of their development and their later expansion. The later historical tradition represents the Etruscans as a confederation of twelve principal cities, and we know that by the fifth century, and probably before, a meeting of the cities took place every spring at the Sanctuary of the god Voltumna in the territory of Volsinii – a national festival with market, games and religious celebrations. It could be made the occasion for political discussion and must always have served to settle matters of dispute between cities on the basis of a common religious law which the Etruscan sacred books are known to have contained.

But even if the religious festival existed as early as the seventh century, it can hardly have represented an effective league or federal government, deliberating and executing common policy. Such a league would be a remarkable anomaly in the period. Our evidence suggests that in the early period there were loosely joined alliances between cities; one story, admittedly dubious, refers to five north Etruscan city-states in support of the Latins against Rome under Tarquinius Priscus. Although the league of twelve traditionally goes back to an early period, the earliest attempt to achieve common action by all the states is referred by Livy to the year 434, when, after the capture of Fidenae, Veii and the Faliscans sent envoys to call a council of the Etruscan peoples. The capture of Veii's Tiber bridgehead was, of course, a serious threat to all the Etruscan people which might be expected to unite their various interests. But most of the time the north Etruscan cities remained aloof from Veii's quarrels with Rome and even helped Rome with grain supplies in time of shortage. Another mighty threat, that of the Gallic invasions, is said to have produced an army drawn from all the Etruscan cities. Some scholars, it should be said, think that the establishment of Etruscan rule in Italy was the result of a great warlike enterprise, and that common effort was maintained into the sixth century with the systematic colonization of the Po valley and Campania. This view stems from the conception of invading Etruscans as a highly organized minority imposing itself by right of conquest on an alien people, a conception which, as we have seen, has no real archaeological foundation.

The seventh century in Etruria is sometimes known as the "orientalizing" period; it is the age of the great tombs of gold like the Regolini-Galassi at Caere. The word "orientalizing" derives from the enormous quantity of objects of eastern origin or inspiration which have been found in the tombs and it is important for the understanding of Etruscan history to establish how these eastern objects reached Etruria, for trade is the vital element in the early relations between Etruria and her neighbours. By the end of the eighth century, the Greeks had established many colonies in southern Italy and Sicily; in the years that followed the foundation of Cumae, the Euboeans gained control of the Straits of Messina by the foundation of Naxos in 734, and later of Zancle and Rhegium. In 733 the Corinthians established Syracuse which was to become the greatest of the western colonies and quickly became a prosperous trading centre. In the last years of the eighth century several colonies were founded along the foot of the peninsula including Croton and the great Sybaris. According to the Greek historians, the Phoenicians had preceded the Greeks as the leading traders in western markets but the tradition has not been confirmed by archaeology. There is no evidence for Phoenician colonization before the Greek, and very little to suggest that they were able to establish a foothold in the Greek sphere of influence until the end of the seventh century. Their colonizing enterprise was confined to the north coast of Africa, where Carthage was founded around 700 B.C., and to Spain, where they colonized and traded widely in metals and were able to resist successfully the challenge of Greek trade led by the Phocaeans.

We must suppose, therefore, that most of the oriental objects from widely different

VENETI

LIGURIANS

Mantua
Adria
R. Po Spina
Felsina (Bologna)
Marzabotto

R. Arno
Florence
Arretium
Volterra
Populonia
Vetulonia
Rusellae
Vulci

ELBA

Alalia

CORSICA

Perugia
Clusium
Volsinii

R. Tiber

UMBRIANS

Tarquinia
Caere Veii
Rome
Praeneste

LATINS

SAMNITES

SARDINIA

Cumae

Capua
Nola

Paestum

Tarentum

Sybaris

Croton

Locri

CARTHAGINIAN COLONIZATION

Zancle

Rhegium

Naxos

GREEK COLONIZATION

Selinus
SICILY
Akragas
Syracuse

ETRUSCAN EXPANSION

Erratum
The key to the shadings should
read in the following order;
Etruscan expansion, Carthaginian
colonization, Greek colonization.

sources came through the intermediary of Greek trade, especially Corinthian trade which largely dominated the Etruscan market for most of the seventh century. Greek ships probably carried the North Syrian, Anatolian, and Phoenician bronzes, the ivory, the gold and silver which flooded in. But we cannot rule out the possibility of more direct eastern contacts as a factor in the development of archaic Etruscan civilization; in north Etruria, especially at Vetulonia, where the quantity of eastern imports is considerable, Greek pottery is comparatively rare, and this suggests that the imports may have reached there from more direct eastern sources. We cannot rule out some oriental immigration during the period, especially after the middle of the seventh century when the Etruscans had established direct trading links with the Carthaginians, as is shown by the large quantity of Etruscan *bucchero* and Italo-Corinthian pottery which has been found at Carthage. There is evidence for craftsmen in gold, ivory and other precious materials coming to Etruria from the eastern Mediterranean. One of Caere's ports was called Punicum, a name which suggests that it was the port specially concerned with Carthaginian trade. In the following century the links with the great Phoenician city were to become even closer.

As Etruria grew in prosperity, the more powerful cities began to contemplate territorial expansion. The events that had established the frontiers of the Etruscan homeland were over. On the east, the Tiber river became the frontier with the Umbrians, but trade with the eastern seaboard of Italy, especially with the Picenes who occupied the country between the Gran Sasso and Ancona, led to early attempts to establish trading posts in Umbrian territory. Many fine Etruscan objects from the mid-sixth century have been found in Umbria, among them the magnificent chariot from Monteleone di Spoleto now in the Metropolitan Museum, New York; it appears

Above left. Faience vase decorated with Egyptian scenes and a cartouche of the Egyptian king, Bocchoris. From a chamber tomb at Tarquinia. *Right.* Parade chariot of wood with bronze fittings, from a tomb at Monteleone di Spoleto

Left. Map of Italy showing Etruscan expansion and Greek and Carthaginian spheres of influence

probable that Todi became an Etruscan town serving as a bridgehead on the Tiber. The Umbrians were traditional enemies of the Etruscans who are said to have superseded them and captured three hundred of their cities; in later times both sides are said to have crossed the river boundary to fight one another. But the Etruscans attempted no massive territorial advance into the Apennine regions and beyond. Instead their earliest territorial ambitions lay towards the south, towards the rich plains of Campania and the Greek colonies. In the Villanovan period there had already been close connections between Etruria and Campania and perhaps some movement of people between the one place and the other. Already in the seventh century the Etruscans may have established trading posts in the area and something like planned Etruscan colonization extending as far south as Salerno had taken place by the end of the century. These moves were the prelude to the great struggle for power between the chief protagonists, the Etruscans, the Greeks and the Carthaginians, which occupied much of the sixth century.

The evidence for early Etruscan territorial expansion into Campania is very strong. By about 625 B.C. Etruscan influence is marked in Latium south of the Tiber. The rich Etruscan graves at Palestrina, which include the famous Barberini and Bernardini tombs, suggest that the upper class of this Latin city was thoroughly "Etruscanized", and the prosperity of the place clearly depended on its controlling position on the land route to the south. An Etruscan-type gold fibula from Praeneste has on it one of the earliest Latin inscriptions, recording the names of the maker and the owner. Veii secured control of Fidenae, the bridgehead on the Tiber; the route to the south led from there to the Palestrina gap and via the Liris valley to Cales, Capua, and Nola. By about 600 (the traditional date is 598 B.C.) the Etruscans had probably planted their first Campanian colony, Capua, which they called Voltumnus; and there was steady expansion until about 540 B.C. when they acquired their southernmost outpost, Pontefratte di Salerno. Here the finds range from about the middle of the sixth century. The southward push in the late seventh century may be connected with the creation of Rome as an Etruscan city and the establishing of the dynasty of the Tarquins. A widespread Etruscan hegemony in Latium is proved by the distribution of place-names of Etruscan origin and the legends of early kings with Etruscan names, like Tarchetio of Alba Longa.

We do not know much about the way in which this Etruscan colonization was achieved, whether by communal effort or by the individual enterprise of powerful

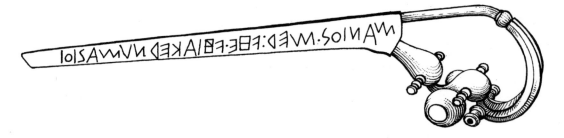

Gold fibula bearing a Latin inscription, from Praeneste

cities. The historical tradition is equivocal; we can hardly accept the story that each of the twelve cities founded its own colony in Campania and, later, in the Po valley, and it would seem more probable that the first southern colonies were planted by the south Etruscan cities. However it was carried out, the effect is clear; it brought the Etruscans into open conflict with the Greek cities and intensified the commercial and naval rivalry between the two powers. The Etruscans now allied themselves more closely with Carthage which since 585 B.C., when Tyre was destroyed by Nebuchadnezzar, controlled the Phoenician colonies of the west; a treaty between the two powers clearly defined their spheres of influence in the Tyrrhenian Sea and the western Mediterranean in general. At this time Etruscan foreign policy looked chiefly to the south, resisting all attempts by Greeks to establish themselves north of the Bay of Naples.

The first half of the sixth century is in many ways the most successful period in Etruscan foreign policy. If relations with the Campanian colonies and with Syracuse were becoming increasingly difficult, flourishing trade was carried on with the prosperous city of Sybaris whose close relations with the Etruscans resulted in a strong Ionian influence on the customs and manners of the Etruscans. The ships of Miletus in Asia Minor brought goods to Sybaris and thence they were carried overland to the Campanian colonies and on by land or sea to Etruria. The turning point came in 540 B.C. when the Phocaeans who had long played a dominant role in western trade and had colonized Marseilles in 600 B.C. were joined by their compatriots who had been driven from their home in Asia by the Persians and attempted to expand their Corsican colony at Alalia, founded in 564. The threat to the Etruscans was obvious, but the action was also a serious threat to Carthage. The Phocaeans may also have been trying to gain a foothold in Sardinia which had become a Carthaginian preserve. Throughout the sixth century there had been an intense struggle between the Greeks and the Carthaginians for the rich metal resources of Spain, and much of the Greek effort had been led by Phocaea which now threatened to establish a powerful new commercial base. In 535 the Etruscans, with Caere apparently playing the major role, formed a military alliance with the Carthaginians, and a combined fleet of 120 vessels fought a battle with a smaller force of Phocaeans who suffered heavy losses and were forced to abandon the island. It is strikingly indicative of the extent of Greek influence at Caere that the colony she then founded on Corsica was called Nicaea, a Greek name, and that when the ruthless stoning of Phocaean prisoners was followed by a plague, it was to the oracle of Delphi that she turned for advice. Caere, it must be remembered, had a Greek name, Agylla, and a treasury in the sanctuary of Apollo at Delphi. Pyrgi, the name of her chief port, is Greek, and Pyrgi is actually said to be a Greek foundation.

But for all Caere's philhellenism, the results of the Battle of Alalia were disastrous for relations between the southern Greek colonies and the Etruscans. The Phocaeans fled south to found a new colony at Elea (Velia) in Lucania. Cumae now began open war with the Etruscan colonies in Campania, Syracuse adopted an implacably anti-Etruscan policy, and the colony of Cnidians on the island of Lipari is recorded as having introduced the Spartan system of military education to combat the menace of Etruscan ships. In 524 B.C. the Etruscans made a massive effort to overcome Cumae. Our ancient source for these events, Dionysius of Halicarnassus, preserves the Greek account, and a very partisan one at that, even for early Greek local history. The Etruscans are said to have amassed a force of 500,000, including 18,000 horse, and to have fought, as barbarians do, in complete disorder. The result was a thorough defeat. There is archaeological evidence for a considerable increase in the number of Etruscans in Campania about this time, and it is to this period that the earliest Etruscan inscriptions, found at Capua, Suessula, Nola and Pompeii, seem to belong.

Not long after the defeat at Cumae, in 508 B.C., the Cumaeans under the tyrant Aristodemus again overcame the Etruscans who were now besieging Aricia in Latium under the command of Porsenna's son, Arruns; the defeat broke Etruscan power in Latium and cut the land routes to the south. Porsenna had just captured Rome in what seems to have been a major Etruscan offensive against the south, sparked off by the expulsion of the Etruscan kings of Rome. Ruler of the powerful northern city of Clusium, Porsenna had apparently established a strong alliance of Etruscan cities and in one tradition is designated king of Etruria. But his efforts do not seem to have succeeded in re-opening the land routes; Rome and the other cities of Latium were achieving an ever-increasing measure of independence. Aristodemus, while vigorously opposing Porsenna, may still have maintained good relations with the maritime states, and actually gave asylum to Tarquin of Rome. The southern colonies, although they survived and apparently achieved a satisfactory *modus vivendi* with the Greeks for another hundred years, never constituted a further threat. In 510 Sybaris had been destroyed by Croton, and with her died a large part of Etruscan prosperity.

The northern expansion of the Etruscans is later than her colonization of the south. From the seventh century onwards, the Etruscans had conducted a flourishing trade with northern Italy. The Villanovans of the Bologna region, lacking the rich resources of raw materials, had developed more slowly than the people of Etruria. They obtained their raw materials and other imports from Etruria, and by their favoured position on the trade routes to the north they shared something of the prosperity of the Etruscan cities. About the middle of the sixth century Etruscan trade with the north began to take on a new impetus, extending its interests to the rich markets of central Europe. We are still not able to assess the volume of this trade. The earliest enterprise by which Mediterranean imports reached central Europe was Greek, led chiefly by the commercial activity of Phocaea, but after the battle of Alalia Phocaean influence declined; the Carthaginians asserted their power along the Spanish coast, while the Etruscans seem to have usurped the markets of central Europe, trading Greek goods and their own with the north. Affinities between the barbarian society of France and the Etruscans are obvious and there was strong Etruscan influence in this area from the late sixth century. The burial of a Hallstatt princess at Vix contains both Greek and Etruscan objects, all of which may have come through Etruria.

The Etruscans seem to have preferred to use the central Alpine passes, and so the control of the Po valley assumed increasing importance in their policy. Another vital factor was the flourishing Greek commerce with the head of the Adriatic. At some time in the sixth century the Greeks had founded a number of trading posts in the area, the most important being Spina on a lagoon some two miles from the sea near the southern estuary of the river Po. The Etruscans determined to take advantage of this Greek trade and there followed a determined effort to colonize parts of the Po valley. The extent of the colonization is uncertain, but there is some evidence that, at its height, it extended over large parts of the Po valley as far as the mountain zone and included a number of settlements on the Adriatic coast from the delta to Pesaro. Marzabotto was established in the Reno valley, the regular line of communications between the Po valley and Etruria; Melpum, Verona and Mantua guarded the entrances to the Alpine passes; Placentia and Cremona controlled crossings of the Po. Mantua, according to Virgil who was born there, was a mixed city which drew its strength from its Etruscan heritage. Trade was not the only factor in this northern Etruscan colonization. It is also clear that the Etruscans successfully exploited the rich agricultural resources of the area by draining the valley and introducing superior methods of husbandry; one of the main objects of the flourishing Athenian trade in the fifth century was to obtain grain supplies.

Of the Etruscan settlements north of the Apennines three only are comparatively well known. Felsina (Bologna) and Marzabotto, whose ancient name is not recorded, were both situated on the ledge of higher ground at the base of the Apennines near the entrance to two comparatively easy Apennine passes. Bologna was particularly well-placed as a centre of communications; southwards were the passes of the Apennines, east and west the old trackways along the Po marshes, and to the north the valley of the Adige leading to the Brenner and to central Europe. Spina, by tradition a Greek city and perhaps in origin a small trading post, seems to have been refounded as an Etrusco-Greek city; it always had a very mixed population and the inscriptions of the fifth and fourth centuries show a very strong Venetic element with Etruscan names comparatively rare. Spina is one of the most fascinating ancient sites. Aerial survey has revealed the main lines of this remarkable town in which the principal streets were waterways; there was a grand canal with minor canals enclosing housing areas in which the houses were built on timber foundations. Its cemeteries, from which over 3,000 tombs have been excavated, are a rich source of fine Greek vases.

The steady worsening of Etrusco-Greek relations in the south at the end of the sixth century drew the Etruscans to a greater concentration of effort on their north-eastern expansion. The whole area of the basins of the Po and Adige rivers, known to the Romans as Cisalpine Gaul, has rich water-meadows and fertile soil. To cultivate it with success requires efficient drainage and irrigation, and there is little doubt that the Etruscans devoted a great deal of effort to achieve a prosperous agriculture in the region. It seems clear that during the great period of Athenian trade with the region, which falls in the years of the Athenian Empire, from 480 to 440 B.C., grain was as much a motive as metals, perhaps the chief motive. In return, the Athenians flooded in their luxury goods, especially their fine red-figure pottery which was so enormously admired in Etruria; the Etruscan market must have become the chief outlet for Athenian potters in the period. The steady increase in this trade is revealed by the statistics of pottery found in Spina's tombs – 63 for the last quarter of the sixth century, 110 for the first quarter of the fifth and 309 for the second quarter.

As in the case of the Campanian colonization, we know very little about the methods by which the Po valley was colonized by the Etruscans. The middle of the sixth century saw the rise to power of Clusium and Vulci and the great commercial prosperity of other inland cities such as Orvieto; one is tempted to connect this prosperity with the development of the northern markets. Vulci, certainly, has yielded by far the largest proportion of Athenian pottery of the late sixth and fifth centuries, and its fine metalwork has been found on the Acropolis at Athens and in other Greek places. It was a colourful and often bloody period in the history of the Etruscan states, and we get a vivid reminder of it in the pictures painted on the walls of the François Tomb at Vulci in the third or second century B.C. A series of pictures shows Vulcian heroes in combat with men from other Etruscan places, a reflection of how Vulcian power was won; we see Macstrna freeing Caile Vipinas from his bonds, Larth Ulthes stabbing Laris Papathnas of Volsinii, Rasa of Vulci overcoming Pesna Arcmsnas of Sovana, Aule Vipinas fighting Venthi Cau(le)s, and Marce Camitlnas, another Vulcian, murdering Cneve Tarchu-(nies), a member of the Tarquin family of Rome. Macstrna is Servius Tullius, apparently, and his exploits with the Vipinas brothers are believed to have achieved the overthrow of Tarquin in Rome and the subsequent rule of Tullius. The Vipinas brothers, though involved in other legendary episodes, are historical figures; the Avile Vipiienas whose name appears on a *bucchero* cup dedicated at Veii in the mid-sixth century may well be our hero, and the account of Macstrna finds archaeological

Landscape at the foot of the Apennines near Bologna

Left. Detail of a painting from the François Tomb, Vulci. The scene shows Marce Camitlnas killing Cneve Tarchunies. *Right*. Etruscan bronze helmet, dedicated at Olympia by Hieron of Syracuse, after his victory over the Etruscans at Cumae in 474 B.C.

confirmation, if nothing else, in the strong Vulcian influence on Rome at the same period. Clusium, meanwhile, was emerging as the most powerful city of the north, soon to play a dominating role in Etruscan history. She may have taken a leading part in the northern expansion (the name of Felsina is linked with a family of Clusium, the Felsnal), and it was she who eventually had to bear the brunt of the Gallic invasions at the end of the fifth century. Thus, while the southern cities declined in power, Clusium and Vulci rose to prominence and it is likely that the northern colonization and the development of trade were vital elements in their rise to prosperity.

The land empire of the Etruscans reached its maximum extent towards the end of the sixth century; the next century saw the steady decline of Etruscan power throughout Italy. In the first half of the century, the Etruscan cities made a vigorous attempt to defend their possessions by land and sea. Carthage remained their ally, but an uncertain one, and in 480 the Carthaginians themselves suffered a terrible defeat at Himera against an alliance of Syracuse under the tyrant Gelon and the city of Akragas which greatly weakened their power. The Etruscans made yet one more attempt to break the power of Cumae but were decisively beaten by the Cumaeans and the Syracusans under Gelon's successor Hieron in a naval battle off Cumae in 474. It was not their only attempt to assert their strength in southern waters against the Syracusans. One of the Etruscan honorific inscriptions from Tarquinia tells of an Etruscan magistrate who led an army into Sicily – the first Etruscan, so the inscription says, to lead troops across the sea – and received the sceptre and gold crown of military triumph. It is tempting to connect this event with the early fifth century when the Etruscans were still capable of a vigorous offensive policy by sea.

In the north, the Etruscans, at least for most of the fifth century, seem to have conducted an effective resistance to the Gauls who threatened their possessions north of the

Apennines. A gravestone from Felsina (Bologna) of the late fifth century showing a combat with a Gaul may be that of a man who fell in resisting the advance of the barbarians at this time. The famous Certosa bronze *situla* (plate 13) contains among its relief-pictures scenes which suggest an efficient military organization in the Po valley to combat the Gaulish menace. A cavalry élite, so vital a part of tactics in the river valley, and three different types of well-drilled infantry soldiers appear in the pictures on this most important document of Etruscan colonial life. We do not know when the first bands of Gaulish tribes, attracted by the prosperity of the Po valley under Etruscan rule, had made their way through the Alpine passes and begun to harry the Etruscan cities, but it is clear that if there was economic depression and decline in Etruria proper, the Po valley continued to prosper well into the second half of the fifth century, and the real crisis did not come until the end of it.

In the second half of the fifth century, the Etruscan states with their sea power largely broken were compelled to resort to an almost purely defensive strategy. They were not able, it seems, to put an effective fleet on the sea or a well-drilled army into the field, and internal dissension added to the problems of many of the city-states. This was the period when the Etruscans began to build strong walls to defend their cities, when the coastal ports were ceaselessly harried by the Greeks, and Rome was making her first inroads into Etruscan territory in the south. In 454 the Syracusans under Phayllus attacked Elba and in the following year sixty triremes under Apelles, ostensibly to put down Etruscan piracy, sacked some of the Etruscan ports and took Elba and Corsica. In 438 the war broke out between Rome and her nearest Etruscan neighbour, Veii. In 432 Capua fell to the Samnites. From this time onwards the Etruscans were reduced to desperate defence of their own homeland, their land empire irretrievably lost. In 396 Veii, the great city which had played so significant a role in early Roman history, fell, and at the same time, according to tradition, the Gauls captured the Etruscan city of Melpum in the Po valley. These two events marked the beginning of the end of Etruscan power in Italy, inaugurating a long period of struggle during which Etruria was absorbed into the expanding empire of Rome. The Etruscan league, if it had ever been the source of effective united action, was now disunited; the great days of the Etruscans were over.

50

Plate 3. Bronze cauldron decorated with lion and griffin *protomai*, and a conical bronze stand with repoussé reliefs of male sphinxes. Cauldron and stand are oriental in form and decoration and may be of oriental workmanship. From the Barberini Tomb, Praeneste. About 630 B.C.
(Villa Giulia, Rome)

Chapter Five

GOVERNMENT AND PEOPLE

Warriors, priests, and producers are the basic elements of a primitive society such as Etruria was in its early period. The warrior aristocracy are the sole proprietors of the land, and at their head is the king, the basis of whose power is command in war. The king is absolute and supreme under the authority of the gods. The picture of a virile warrior society emerges from all our evidence about early Etruria. In some versions of the mythology of early Rome, one of the three tribes originates with Lucumo and his men, who are specialists in the art of war, engaged as such by Romulus; Lucumo is the Roman word for an Etruscan city king, derived apparently from a good Etruscan word – *lauchme*. The splendid burials of early Etruscan warriors, with their evidence of abundant wealth, recreate for us a vivid picture of the pomp and splendour of early Etruscan society. In the Regolini-Galassi tomb at Caere we have the burial of one of the great lords of Caere, perhaps its king. He lay in death armed as a warrior and surrounded by his wealth; buried near him was his consort in her gold embroidered robes amid her rich possessions. The ancient tradition attributes to Etruria many of the ceremonies and trappings of Roman public life, believing that much of the dress and ceremonial originally belonged to Etruscan kings. The king sat in an ivory chair, wore a gold crown and carried a sceptre surmounted by an eagle; his tunic was of purple edged with gold and he wore an embroidered cloak of purple. He was accompanied by attendants called lictors who carried a ceremonial axe bound with rods, the symbol of absolute power over life and death. The Tarquins of Rome may be thought of as typical Etruscan kings; they were chief justices, army leaders and high priests.

The military basis of early Etruscan society is certain. In most Etruscan places there is a steady increase in the quantity of arms and armour from the earliest Villanovan graves, and after the middle of the eighth century male burials, especially the richest, are often accompanied by a great show of military power. The richest burials are sometimes chariot burials, such as have been found in Caere, Populonia, and Marsiliana; the king, it appears, and some of the nobles went into battle in war chariots, though chariot fighting is unlikely in the period. The horse-owning aristocracy fought as cavalry; horses' bits, harness pieces and the like are common finds, and the horse is a frequent motif on the funerary equipment in the richer tombs. The series of tripod-bowls found at Tarquinia, Vetulonia and Veii show helmeted cavalry-men. The development of a heavily armed infantry can also be followed in the graves. While the earliest Villanovan burials have arms of various kinds, the only defensive armour is the helmet; but in the course of the eighth century the repertory of arms increases and body armour of Greek type becomes more common. The weapons are now chiefly of iron; arrow-heads are rare, suggesting that the bow was little used. By the sixth century B.C.

Plate 4. Miniature bronze groups from the decoration of a helmet showing Hercules fighting with Achelous, horsemen riding down a fallen warrior, and two centaurs overcoming Kaineus. Made probably in Vulci and found at Orvieto. Late sixth century B.C. (Ny Carlsberg Glyptotek, Copenhagen)
Plate 5. Three *bucchero* vessels. Late seventh century B.C. (British Museum, London)

Left. Bronze breastplate of an Etruscan heavy-armed warrior. *Right.* Gravestone of Avele Feluske, found at Vetulonia

the Etruscans could put into the field an efficient body of troops wearing body armour of Greek type and fighting in close formation with thrusting spears, swords and daggers, and supported by a cavalry arm drawn mainly from the upper classes.

We can say little of the military organization of early Etruria. The supreme command lay with the king; his nobles commanded the various detachments which were probably recruited by them on a basis of feudal obligation. There cannot have been a large standing army, but kings may have had bodies of retainers permanently at arms and commanded by professional soldiers. The foot soldiers were originally clients of the king and nobles; in early Rome and probably in many of the cities of Etruria during historical times a free peasantry formed the nucleus of the army. The military commanders of early days are represented by the splendid figure of Avele Feluske on the stone which stood over his tomb at Vetulonia, dating from the late seventh century. In his hand he carries a double axe, the symbol of his authority; he wears a helmet and is armed with a big round shield. According to the most plausible interpretation of the accompanying inscription, the stone was set up by Hirumina of Perugia (?), a comrade in arms. Feluske has been thought of as a typical "Condottiere", representative of a class of professional soldier who served the city rulers of the day. However this may be, he is an intriguing figure from the colourful military life of early Etruria, of whose exploits we would dearly like to know more, and of whose prowess in the art of war there can be no doubt.

The Etruscans' early exploits on the sea suggest that the coastal cities could put considerable numbers of ships of war and armed merchantmen to sea to harry the trading ships of their rivals or defend themselves against piratical attacks. The well-known Aristonothos *krater* of the late seventh century found at Caere is the work of a Greek artist and shows what may be an encounter between a Greek ship and an Etruscan privateer. The Etruscan vessel has a deep keel with the bow and stern both rising from the water and is strikingly different in design from the Greek; both vessels are manned by armed warriors who are preparing to engage as the vessels close. The Etruscans, though armed very similarly to the Greeks, are distinguishable by their massive body shields which reach almost to their ankles. The Etruscans, in the days when they were serious rivals to the Greeks in the northern waters of the Tyrrhenian Sea, must have been able to put their fighting ships to sea at short notice, and Caere must have had something like a standing navy, commanded by those nobles of the city whose interests lay in foreign trade and commerce. The military protection required for vessels sailing in the Mediterranean in order to conduct any kind of successful trade in piratical days would tend to keep the control of commerce in the hands of the lords of the cities.

The king's power did not rest on military command alone, for he was also the chief priest and his rule was under the divine authority of the gods; it was he who possessed the chief power to provoke the gods to declare their will towards men. Etruscan religion, of which we know a good deal, was based upon the careful observance of an elaborate prescribed ritual. The Lucumones, we are told, learnt the revelations of this religion from a certain Tages, a divine child with the wisdom of age who was once ploughed out of the ground by a farmer of Tarquinia; a nymph, Vegoia, also got the credit for some of the revelation. The secrets of this revealed religion and its observances

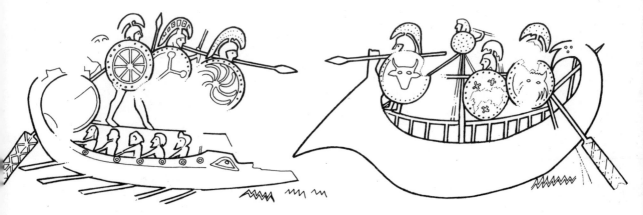

A sea battle, drawn from a painted vessel, the so-called Aristonothos *krater*, found at Caere

were jealously guarded by the kings and nobles; it was they alone who could interpret the signs of thunder, examine the entrails of sacrificial beasts, seek out and consider the portents, and so understand the will of the gods. A body of skilled priests, drawn, no doubt, from the aristocratic families, soon came into being, subordinated to the king's authority but becoming increasingly important as the life of the cities grew more complex. Their intimate knowledge of prescribed rituals, which were nowhere written down, and the aura of mystery that surrounded them were given outward expression in their symbols of authority – the curved staff, the cap, the axe, the knife. Control of the priesthood was the cornerstone of the king's power. As we know from references to the ritual books of the Etruscans, codified at a later period, every activity of human life was governed by religious rules. The secrets of this practical religion covered no less than the whole administration of the states.

Our picture of early Etruria, then, is of a people dominated by a military aristocracy under the rule of kings. The ruling class controlled the land and every activity of Etruscan life, commanding the obedience of a people who were without rights and privileges. The nobles, whose tombs make a striking contrast with those of the common people, kept in their hands the mineral, agricultural and commercial wealth of the cities. The status of the producers, as in all primitive societies, can have been little better than that of slave, though it must in fact have been distinguished from that of the true slaves who thronged the houses of the nobles and ministered to their every need, for these were mostly foreigners captured in war or purchased through the flourishing slave-markets of the day.

The position of the common people in Etruria has been much discussed. Dionysius of Halicarnassus, writing in the time of the Emperor Augustus, compares their lot with that of the feudal serfs in certain backward parts of Greece and contrasts it with that of the rulers in whose hands the power lay. The picture that Dionysius gives must accord fairly well with the state of affairs in the early period of the Etruscan cities but it seems certain that in many cities, especially the progressive coastal cities, a process of revolutionary change began at an early period, with the result that a more broadly-based society was ultimately developed. It would be wrong to think that this development took place everywhere, or that the political history of all the cities was the same. At Veii, for example, in the late fifth century, we find the power still in the hands of kings when most of the other cities had certainly given up monarchic rule. Nor need the causes of revolutionary changes be always the same; in one city, military reform may lie at the basis of it, in another, the development of commercial interests, in another the preaching of political reform. And it is probably true that many of the Etruscan states remained, in some sense, archaic communities lacking the flexibility of contemporary Greek city-states. Valerius Maximus tells the story of a political revolution at Volsinii in the third century where the people of the city, represented as slaves, were handed the reins of power by the decadent aristocracy and proceeded to abuse that power most ruthlessly.

Economic development was among the chief causes of political change. Etruscan prosperity had been derived from a soundly based local trade in manufactured goods between cities and a flourishing export of raw materials. This early trade was conducted by barter. In the eighth and seventh centuries the Etruscan cities were trading arms

Bronze figure, perhaps an Etruscan augur carrying the curved staff (*lituus*), his emblem of office

and luxury goods with the Picenes of the eastern seaboard in return for amber and other commodities; with the Greeks they were exchanging raw metal for pottery, textiles, oil, wine and so on. In the early period the narrow aristocracy who monopolized political power under the kings were also the chief exploiters of commerce and industry, but inevitably the expansion of trade in the course of the sixth century made their position increasingly difficult to maintain. The development of trade and colonization released new forces in the politics of the states, chiefly by creating a flourishing class of merchants outside the circle of the old exclusive hereditary groups. The effect of this, though we have very little direct evidence, must have been much the same as in the Greek city-states, with increasing agitation for political rights by a commercial middle class. As in Greece, the result may have been the rise of tyrants, absolute rulers who came to power with the support of the discontented elements of the population. Such a one may have been the Thefarie Velianas whose name and title are preserved on the gold plaques found at Pyrgi. He held the office of *zilath*, the principal magistracy, and at the time of the inscription was in his third year of office. In one view that larger-than-life character, Porsenna of Clusium, was a political dictator rather than a king; he was certainly one of the most powerful rulers of Etruscan history with a reputation for wealth and megalomania which recalls the tyrants of Greek history.

The progress of social revolution is reflected in many of the cemeteries of Etruria. The contrast in the early period between the massive tumuli of kings and nobles and the modest interments of the people yields place to groups of less ostentatious tombs, suggesting a more broadly-based upper class. At Orvieto, a town whose ancient name remains unknown, the cemetery known as the Crocefisso del Tufo was developed in the late sixth century and laid out in a regular plan with modest chamber tombs jostling one another. Most of the tombs, of which some 300 have been explored, are similar in form and often have lintels inscribed with the name of the head of the family. They look very much like the tombs of a prosperous middle class with little trace of wide social gulfs – a merchant class, perhaps, rising to prominence in the sixth century through the favoured commercial position of the town. The whole pattern of a colonial settlement such as Marzabotto, established about the same time, suggests that the colonizers were modest folk with a stake in the commercial enterprise of the place, backed by an efficient military organization to defend it.

Politically the result of the social revolution must have been that in most of the Etruscan cities the old monarchy and the tribal aristocracy disappeared in the course of the sixth and fifth centuries, giving place to a more broadly based oligarchic form of government. Elected magistrates performed the functions of the kings, coming from the ranks of a ruling class – the Etruscan *principes* of the Roman historical tradition – whose assembly would form the main deliberative council of the city. The class of the *principes* was probably a large and cosmopolitan social class of varied origins, literate, educated and prosperous. The Etruscans, who must be numbered among the most receptive of all ancient societies to foreign influences, were never exclusive. The most famous of foreigners accepted into Etruscan society was a Corinthian aristocrat, Demaratus, who settled in Tarquinia in the seventh century and married an Etruscan noblewoman. Demaratus was, no doubt, a representative of a large class of resident aliens, mostly Greeks but perhaps of other nationalities, who settled in Etruscan cities

Chamber tombs in the cemetery of Crocefisso del Tufo, Orvieto

from an early period. Buried in a rich orientalizing tomb at Tarquinia was a man of mixed Etrusco-Greek stock, son of a Greek father, his name Rutile Hipucrates (Hippocrates). Greek merchants and craftsmen must have thronged the cities.

Commercial interests were by no means the only cause of reform and change. In Rome the mainspring of early social and political reform was military, and military service was the basis of the claim to citizenship. The great reforms designed to reinforce the army with plebeian recruits and reorganize its tactics were attributed to Servius Tullius, who in the version of the Etruscans was, as we have seen, a hero of Vulci. It is not impossible that similar reforms had already been introduced in his native Vulci which, with Clusium, became one of the most powerful cities in Etruria in the middle of the sixth century. Such a hypothesis would help to explain the much more rapid social and political advance of certain cities in contrast with those which rejected democratic change and still adhered to the prevailing system of serfdom.

By the end of the period with which we are concerned, a republican form of government had been established in most of the states with the chief magistrates elected annually like the consuls of Rome. The *zilath* (the word appears to have several variants: *zilat, zilath, zilac, zilach*) was the chief magistrate and there were a number of lower offices, though our evidence for their names is drawn entirely from inscriptions of a later period, mostly from the third century B.C. Even in that period magistrates' inscriptions come from a limited number of cities. It may be that there were several *zilaths*, forming a collegiate body, but with one chief magistrate among them; certainly in later times the office was reached through a number of subordinate offices and priesthoods, which include those of *maru* and *purthne*. The chief magistrates frequently came from the country towns of the city-states; the man of Norchia who appears on one of the honorific inscriptions set up in the Roman period at Tarquinia has already been mentioned, and we hear of another Tarquinian *zilath* who was a native of Musarna. The *zilath* (or chief *zilath*) assumed the functions of the king, taking over his command in war and his chief administrative authority. In one of the Tarquinian inscriptions we hear of a *zilath* (the word is translated as *praetor*) who led an Etruscan army into Sicily and was rewarded with the sceptre, the eagle, and the gold crown. The political development of most of the Etruscan cities may have been strikingly like that which took place in Rome when the Republic was established on the expulsion of the Tarquins and the consuls took over the chief functions of the king.

The central government controlled the whole territory of the city-state including many smaller towns and village centres as well as frontier posts and other military sites. It seems fairly clear that in the sixth century a large number of prosperous early sites lost their independence, and that there was considerable movement of population into the big cities. From this time on the increasing administrative problems of the central government probably gave a large measure of autonomy to those settlements that were some distance from the capital and this autonomy increased as the central authority declined. In 386, for example, we find the town of Nepi which was subject to Veii negotiating its own treaty with Rome, without reference to the mother city. In the later period several of the smaller towns had their own magistrates, with the same names as those of the big cities. Apart from the increasing weakness of the chief cities, the important role played by many of the smaller places in the defensive strategy of the states must have raised them to a position of increasing importance, while their landed gentry continued to play a significant role in central political life.

The view that it was the failure to create a free and respectable citizen body which accounted for the ultimate downfall of the Etruscans has been emphatically propounded in the past and still has its adherents among historians today. The view needs to be modified and can scarcely be applied to all the Etruscan states. We may suggest that in the prosperous coastal cities something like a successfully integrated society was developed where the rights of the people, including those of foreign immigrants, were protected by responsible magistrates. An Ionian Greek could set up shop at Caere as free citizen in the sixth century and carry on a flourishing business as a manufacturer of pottery in an atmosphere from which he could draw genuine inspiration. We have evidence for a changing society with slow but steady social reform. If old families tended to survive in power, new elements came inevitably to the fore. In other

Plate 6. Stone figure of a sphinx which once guarded the entrance to an Etruscan tomb near Clusium. About 550 B.C. (Museo Civico, Chiusi)
Overleaf Plate 7. Wall painting of wrestlers; the three metal bowls placed between them are the prizes. From the Tomb of the Augurs, Tarquinia. About 530 B.C.

places, perhaps, the tradition of the Etruscan failure to incorporate the peasant class into public life may be true; the apparent lack of an efficient citizen army in times of greatest crisis would seem to confirm the view. The Romans certainly believed that the greater part of the population of Etruria always remained in a condition of slavery, but it is a late and unfavourable tradition, remembering, perhaps, the days of forced labour under the Tarquins and applying the same conditions indiscriminately to all Etruscan communities. In any case, the slaves who served the high society of Etruria and are shown on the walls of the tombs performing a host of tasks from entertaining the guests with music and dance to work in the kitchen must be distinguished from the mass of the population who worked the mines or ploughed the fields just as their ancestors had done for centuries.

We need to know much more about the political and social organization of the states and the character of the colonial settlements before we can judge the success or failure of Etruscan rule. The conception of an unhealthy body politic overreaching itself in its ambitions is probably just another of those simplifications which have marred our judgment of the Etruscans. By 400 B.C., when the struggle for political rights by the *plebs* of Rome had hardly begun, the Etruscan cities were already in decline and the period of their great prosperity was over. We should be doing the Etruscans far less than justice if we ignored the fact that some of the most important steps in social and political reform which took place in Rome were taken when the city was still ruled by Etruscan kings. When we look at the early history of Etruria it is easy to forget how much had already been achieved, and how rapidly, in the transformation from the primitive feudal community; and how much the whole history of Italy owed to the Etruscans in the political as well as in every other field.

Plate 8. Clay vessel, one of the so-called Caeretan *hydriae*; found in fragments in a tomb at Caere. About 530 B.C. (British Museum, London)

Chapter Six

CITIES AND TOWNS

Of the famous Etruscan cities, the majority are virtually unexplored, and some of them, now overlaid by modern towns, will never be available for excavation. Of the others we know so far what has been discovered by casual or strictly limited excavation and only very general conclusions can be drawn about their appearance. At Caere we have no more than the remains of the circuit of walls, the exits of the principal streets and the sites of one or two temples. At some places, for example, Clusium, almost everything that has been found belongs to the Roman period; at Vetulonia, too, the scant remains of the houses and the city layout belong to the latest period of the city's life. But the prospects for the future are promising. Soon Vulci, until now scarcely more than the victim of looting and disordered excavation, may be thoroughly explored; systematic excavation, which has already achieved important results, is in progress on the site of Rusellae, which looks likely to be the first of the old Etruscan cities whose development we shall understand in detail. Preliminary surveys are being carried out on a number of the smaller towns and settlements within the territories of the city-states. The only Etruscan town whose layout is, at present, known in some detail can scarcely be considered as typical of the chief cities; this is the colonial settlement of Marzabotto, 15 miles south of Bologna. Part of it was excavated about a hundred years ago; work has recently been restarted and is still going on.

The initial development of the Etruscan cities took place, as we have seen, in the late eighth and seventh centuries when the Villanovan settlements were transformed into single communities. The sites were generally well, sometimes spectacularly, defended by nature, with the most easily defensible area serving as an acropolis in time of trouble; man-made defences were often added to strengthen the acropolis but the whole area of settlement was not generally enclosed in artificial defences. At Poggio Buco, an important early site in the valley of the Albegna, the inhabited area is an isolated plateau, most vulnerable on the west side where the natural ditch was apparently excavated deeper; the southern end of the site formed the acropolis and this was isolated by an artificial ditch and mound. At Veii the defences of the acropolis, known as the Piazza d'Armi, seem to have formed a separate system even in a late period when the whole of the city area was enclosed in walls. It is now becoming clear that some of the cities were given a circuit of defensive walls at quite an early period. At Rusellae the earliest stone walls, two miles in circumference, were apparently built in the first half of the sixth century, and there was certainly an earlier defensive system of sun-dried brick, perhaps as early as the seventh century. There may have been other instances. But the walls of squared masonry, generally backed by earthen ramparts, which eventually protected most of the Etruscan cities, belong to the end of the period we are

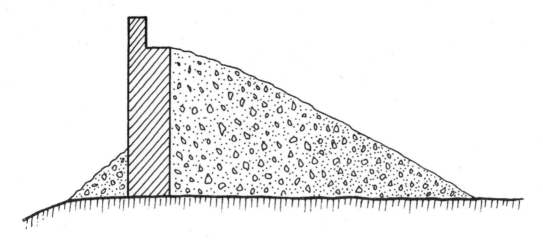

Section of the defences of earth and stone at Veii

dealing with, when the cities were subjected to attacks from the Gauls and Romans and began to fall back on a defensive policy. Before the middle of the fifth century the inhabitants of Veii did not feel the need for any defensive system except the acropolis of Piazza d'Armi. The defences, when built, consisted of an earthen rampart more than 75 feet wide and about 18 feet high with a wall of squared tufa masonry emerging as a vertical breastwork halfway up the forward face of the rampart. The use of massive irregular blocks of masonry in wall-building, the so-called Cyclopean technique, belongs largely to the period of Roman rule in central Italy.

It must not be supposed that the whole area finally occupied by the cities and enclosed in their later walls was built on from the first. In the eighth century the sites of the later cities were probably occupied by groups of Villanovan huts, perhaps isolated from one another in some way. The existence of distinct groups is suggested by the fact that the settlement area was surrounded by a series of quite separate cemeteries. The Villanovan huts followed a fairly uniform design which we know both from the clay models used as cremation urns (plate 1) and from actual remains. The huts might be circular, elliptical, or rectangular, the last form being the most common. The walls were of wattle and daub supported by upright posts; a door in one of the narrow sides was formed by posts and might have a rudimentary porch under a lean-to roof. The rafters were fixed to a long curved beam, supported by a central post, the roof having, in embryo, a triple pitch. There were windows, sometimes as many as three, and holes in the roof to allow the smoke to escape. A certain amount of regional variation may be deduced from the hut-urns; those of Vulci, for example, seem to have deeper overhanging roofs. On an urn of the eighth century from Tarquinia the walls widen out towards the top; there is a wide rectangular window and a circular hole in the roof for the smoke to escape. All the huts were brightly painted, and there is some suggestion of an early taste for ornament, including figured ornament on walls and timbers.

In the seventh century, as the cities developed from the Villanovan villages, the haphazard arrangement of the huts must have been superseded by a more regular layout. The taste for a formal plan with buildings of basically rectangular shape aligned

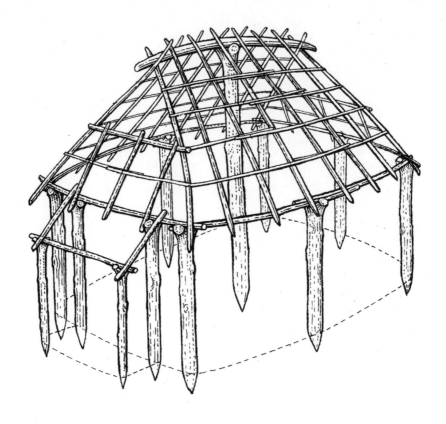

Reconstruction of the "Hut of Romulus" on the Palatine Hill, Rome

upon straight streets is apparent from a fairly early period. On the Piazza d'Armi, the acropolis of Veii, the huts were superseded by a layout with a system of wide crossing streets leading to a sort of piazza, and at Tarquinia there is some evidence of early streets laid out approximately east-west and north-south. By the end of the century wattle-and-daub huts must have been replaced by buildings of more solid structure with foundations of squared stone and walls of timber and plaster, and there must have been a good deal of substantial masonry building, especially of terrace walls to create level areas for development. The area known as the Macchia Grande on the north side of Veii has remains of early houses with their foundations partly cut in the rock and partly built of solid walls; one house has a large rectangular room and a vestibule. At Tarquinia a massive revetment wall was built in the sixth century on the south flank of the city terrace to support a shrine. Of the buildings within the cities during this period we have almost no evidence. The architectural elements of the great seventh century tombs suggest that there was already some impressive public and private building within the cities. The interior arrangements of the tombs of the next century throw a good deal of light on the development of house plans in early Etruria. The earliest houses were probably single-room dwellings of oblong shape adapted from the old hut form, but of more durable structure. New and more complex plans were worked

Painted clay cinerary urn of house form

out in the sixth century, a development which can be followed to some extent in the tombs of the big tumuli at Caere, where the layout is certainly based on the dwellings of the living.

The early part of the sixth century was the period of most rapid growth in the great cities of Etruria, and to this period belongs the earliest evidence we have for Etruscan temple-building. In origin the Etruscan sanctuary was simply an enclosed space laid out to a prescribed form from which portents could be observed; within the sanctuaries were altars of sacrifice to the gods which in the sixth century took on a characteristic rectangular form with heavy base and crowning mouldings. The building of temples to serve as houses of the gods came when Etruscan religion had adopted the anthropomorphism of the Greeks and had built cult-statues of their divinities. The oldest votive material from the Portonaccio site at Veii is of the seventh century B.C. but the earliest temple was not built until the sixth. The first temple on the Manganello site at Caere dates back to about 600 B.C. It is argued plausibly that the earliest Etruscan temple plans derive from the simple hut forms; a rectangular chamber with a little porch. There is, in fact, a good deal of variety in the earliest plans. The temple on Piazza d'Armi at Veii is a simple rectangular shape, 50½ feet long by 26½ feet wide, and the early temple on the Poggio Casetta site at Bolsena is a rectangular room (26 feet long

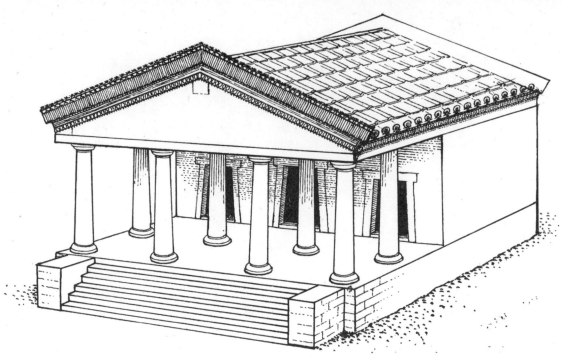

Model of an Etruscan temple of the fifth century B.C.

by 21½ feet wide) within an enclosure 56 feet wide and 43½ feet deep. These temple buildings soon came to occupy a dominating position within the sanctuaries, set against the rear wall and standing on a high base or podium constructed of a network of foundation walls contained in a solid frame. The superstructure was built of wood with protective facings of terracotta slabs, richly decorated with painted reliefs. The design and decoration of the Etruscan temple came under strong Greek influence in the sixth century; the columnar porch was adopted and the whole decoration inspired by Greek models.

Vitruvius, the Roman architect writing in the time of the Emperor Augustus, lays down precise rules for the design of an Etruscan temple. It should be almost square on plan, he says, and divided in depth into two parts of which the front part is occupied by a porch and the rear by three parallel rooms, the central one being the widest, or by a single room flanked by what he calls *alae* (wings). Vitruvius thought there should be four columns on the front with one return column on either side, on the line of the outer wall, and he goes on to prescribe a detailed series of proportions for the columns and superstructure. What Vitruvius gives us is an academic codification of what may be called an "Etrusco-Roman" temple in a late stage of its development, and there has been a good deal of discussion about the origin and development of the type. The most plausible answer to the problem seems to be that originally there was much variety in Etruscan temple forms with the simple rectangular building within an enclosure the prevailing form. A separate tradition perhaps originates with a large room open at the front and containing two or three divisions in its rear part, as appears in a house model from Velletri. This second type, with the addition of a Greek-inspired columnar architecture, could be the origin of the developed form that Vitruvius describes. The recent excavations at Pyrgi, in the most important sanctuary yet discovered in Etruria, have thrown new light on the subject of Etruscan temples. Two temples have been discovered of which one, Temple B, was at first thought to be Greek in design. The second temple, Temple A, built around 470–460 B.C., is similar in form to the temple described by Vitruvius, with a front and back part equal in size, the back part having three parallel chambers; it had magnificent terracotta sculptures of Greek subject and style. The design of Temple A is basically the same as that of the Portonaccio temple at Veii from which the famous Apollo of Veii comes. In both the Pyrgi temples the unit of measurement was the Attic foot. There is no early evidence for Vitruvius's second type of Etruscan temple with *alae*, but it seems to have existed in the fourth century.

Temples, often of very grand scale, must have been the most striking buildings of the early Etruscan cities. The columns were generally of wood, sometimes of stone, with simple unfluted shafts, torus bases and cushion capitals related to Greek Doric. The superstructure was always of wood, faced with terracotta. The architraves were covered with slabs of terracotta forming a continuous frieze generally decorated with figures or ornament; the subjects of the figured friezes might be processions of horsemen, chariot races, assemblies of gods. Beam ends were decorated with terracotta plaques and there was usually a richly ornamented gutter. Other characteristic details were figured ends of the ridge tiles and acroterial groups. In the fifth century the repertory was increased by sculpture in the triangular space of the tympanum. Temple A at Pyrgi, dating from 470–60 B.C., had sculpture in this position fixed to a wooden backing. Much of the terracotta decoration is repetitive, made in moulds; all of it was richly coloured with a basic scheme of black, red and white to which light blue, violet, green and ochre were added. The colour schemes are uninhibited – one can have blue horses or horses with different coloured legs – and the whole effect was rich and colourful.

Apart from temples no other public buildings have survived from the Etruscan cities, but there must have been many splendid private dwellings of the kings and nobles, no less lavish in their decoration and fittings. The development of more complex house plans is clear from the evidence of sixth-century tombs. A number of tomb chambers at Caere dating from the end of the sixth century combine a large central hall with a room opening off the centre of its rear wall flanked by two further rooms. This scheme has something in common with the design of the later Roman house with its *atrium* giving access to the *tablinum* flanked by *alae*; Vitruvius, in fact, calls one type of Roman *atrium*, the *atrium tuscanicum*. Varro derives the word *atrium* itself from Atria, the Etruscan colony on the Adriatic, and the word *athre*, perhaps its Etruscan form, does actually occur, though in an uncertain context, in the famous late-Etruscan religious text of the Zagreb mummy-wrapping. The shape of the central room in these early Etruscan tombs is, however, quite different from the later *atrium*, being wide in proportion to its depth. There is no early example of the characteristic opening of the roof, the *impluvium*, nor any suggestion of the structural forms associated with Vitruvius' *atrium tuscanicum*. But the general link between the Roman house and the axial planning of the early Etruscan house seems to be clear.

The Tomb of the Greek Vases at Caere gives a good idea of the early Etruscan

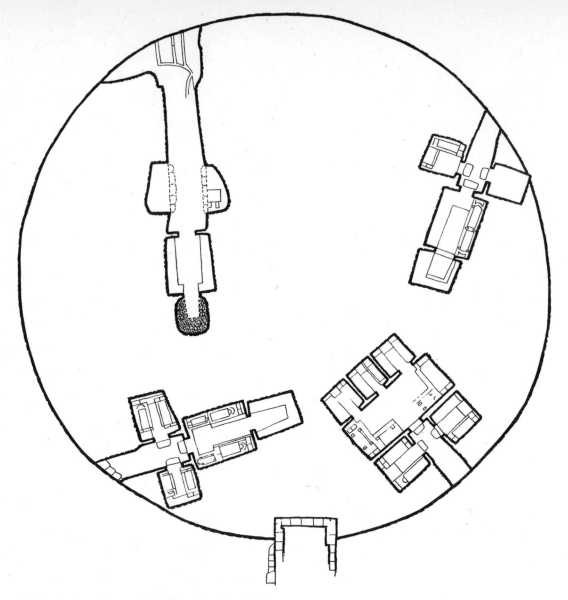

Ground plan of the tombs in Tumulus II at Caere

layout, and in the Tomb of the Capitals, also at Caere, there are two columns with "Aeolic" capitals in the central hall. These tombs also have carved doors and windows derived from domestic architecture, and other elements of interior design and decoration; the characteristic doorway is T-shaped with sloping jambs and the windows are usually square. There is some evidence that the forms of Greek architecture, especially the Doric order which prevailed in Greece during the period, were known in the cities of the south and may have been used by the philhellene Etruscans in the detail of their houses. It may be supposed, too, that pure Greek buildings were erected at such places as Tarquinia, though the Etruscans, unlike the Greeks, never felt the need to express themselves through precisely defined architectural form, nor did they adopt stone monumental architecture on a large scale.

As far as we can tell, the process of urbanization in the great Etruscan cities was comparatively slow at first. There was probably an energetic burst of building activity around 600 B.C. when close attention was paid to all the amenities of urban life. It is difficult to picture the cities' appearance from the evidence we have. Some areas were probably laid out with a regular street plan; the rest might be the result of a more haphazard growth. One modern archaeologist would compare the old Etruscan cities with the "old, charming and disordered Tuscan towns of today", but we might guess that they were less crowded with large parts not built up and therefore more open in appearance. Here and there was a sanctuary with a splendid temple; the houses were simple but colourful with a few outstanding in scale and decoration. Somewhere there must have been areas given over to public assembly and places where games and festivals were held, without permanent buildings; these would be in open areas where temporary booths and seating could be erected, and might at other times be given over to markets. In public places monuments and statues would commemorate the great of the city. It is worth remembering that two thousand bronze statues are supposed to have been plundered from Volsinii by the Romans in 264. The urban amenities would probably compare favourably with any of the cities of the Greek world. Close attention was paid to drainage which kept the city dry and healthy; Clusium's subsoil has a complicated system of sewers and vaulted chambers, the so-called Labyrinth of Porsenna, which may go back to an early period of the city's history. The 25,000 or so people who lived in a city such as Caere could enjoy greater comfort than the inhabitants of most of the cities of the Greek world.

A primitive city must be protected by divinities, aided by human ritual and magic; a magic circle must enclose it. The erudition of the late Republic in Rome attributed to the Etruscans a very elaborate ritual for the founding of cities, drawn, it would seem, from Etruscan ritual books. The detail of the tradition does not, of course, go back to the earliest period of the Etruscan cities which grew up haphazardly, but it does seem to be inspired by developments in Etruscan planning which took place in the sixth century and may to some extent be followed in the Etruscan colonial settlements of the period. While many of its ideas are deep-rooted in the Etruscan conception of city life, much of the Roman tradition was probably fathered on the Etruscans simply because the Romans accepted the general cultural primacy of Etruria in early Italian history. Varro

End wall of the Tomb of the Chairs and Shields at Caere

says that the Romans laid out their towns in accordance with Etruscan ritual; indeed Rome itself had been planned by Romulus with the aid of augural specialists from Etruria. The augurs took the auspices and fixed the main lines of the plan which was based upon the Etruscan doctrine of the divisions of the sky; they established a parallel to the fourfold division of the heavens by setting up two ideal axes at right angles, one east to west following the sun and the other north to south on the main axis of the heavens. The founder of the city, with covered head, then cut the first furrow of the circuit with a plough drawn by a bull and a heifer and the earth was cast on the inside. When he came to the site of a gate he lifted his plough. Traditionally there should be three gates and three temples, with the chief one sited on high ground which gave the best view for augury.

However efficient and thorough the Etruscans may have been as land surveyors and however many elements of the tradition may originate in Etruscan practice, the whole account as we have it is, like Vitruvius' Etruscan temple, a rationalization of a long process of development based, no doubt, on the final codification of the Etruscan ritual books. We have seen that from an early period, certainly from the sixth century B.C., there was a tendency to axial planning in the old cities; at an early period, no doubt, fairly precise rules were laid down for the layout of sanctuaries and the orientation of temple buildings which may have influenced the tradition of axiality and symmetry in public building generally. By the late sixth century regular planning of new areas was a fairly established practice. This is particularly clear in some of the cemeteries of the

Foundations of Etruscan houses at Marzabotto

great cities laid out in the period. The striking feature of the Crocefisso del Tufo cemetery at Orvieto is its regular plan with the tombs built in plots defined by crossing streets; similar tendencies can be seen in those parts of the Banditaccia cemetery at Caere that were laid out in the late sixth century. But the best evidence for developed Etruscan town-planning comes from the colonial settlements established in the second half of the sixth century, especially those of the Po valley. Marzabotto, about 17 miles south of Bologna, is often called the Etruscan Pompeii. It was founded towards the end of the sixth century and since it was excavated some 100 years ago has been taken as the classic example of Etruscan town planning; the earliest occupation goes back to about 540 B.C. but the layout belongs to the end of the century. The town, which has a circuit of about two miles, occupies a level terrace called the Pian di Misano, and is laid out to a strictly axial plan oriented to the chief points of the compass. One broad street, over 50 feet wide, runs from north to south and is crossed by three streets aligned east to west. A series of narrower north–south streets divides the whole area of the town into long rectangular building plots. The temples and sacred buildings on a height to the west of the main terrace are aligned on the same axis.

The same principles as we see in Marzabotto were apparently applied in several other Etruscan colonial settlements. Capua, the colony in Campania, has a series of horizontal streets and vertical divisions creating the building plots, and recently the main lines of a similar layout at Spina have been revealed by aerial photography. The city, which is about 875 acres in area, has, like Venice, canals for streets; the plan is

The site of Spina, showing the lines of the Etruscan canals beneath the modern drainage system

essentially similar, with a grand canal, in fact a canalized branch of the Po, and a series of narrower canals to form the *insulae*. The houses here were built on foundations of timber beams. In all these cases the layout, so far as we can see, is not the one attributed to the Etruscans by the Romans but a form derived from Greek principles of planning associated with the name of Hippodamus, the basic elements of which are the series of horizontal streets and vertical divisions forming the long narrow plots. It seems fairly clear that the Etruscans, in fact, learnt this type of planning from the Greeks in southern Italy; Hippodamus, it may be remembered, was a Milesian and the Etruscans had particularly close relations with this Asiatic city through Sybaris. The pattern is indistinguishable from that of the Greek cities in the same period and does not, apparently, bear any relation to the traditional "Etrusco-Roman" scheme of two axial crossing streets, for which no evidence can so far be found from the older Etruscan sites.

Marzabotto was a well-organized town. A skilful drainage system, making use of the natural slope of the terrace, kept the city dry. The wide principal streets were well paved and equipped with pavements and stepping-stones to cross. Within the long narrow *insulae* the houses were simply built, with foundations of river boulders bedded in clay and a superstructure of partly fired brick walls and tiled timber roofs. The house plans vary a good deal: one scheme has a paved courtyard surrounded by rooms which may have served more than one family. The courtyard was entered from the street by a long corridor and each courtyard had a well. These houses had at least one upper storey and were generally flat-roofed. On the main north–south street there was a frontage of shops in some of which there was evidence of metal industry. Marzabotto must have been a healthy town and as pleasant a place to live in as most ancient cities of the period.

Although we cannot find evidence for the type of planning that the Romans specifically attributed to the Etruscans, it is clear that under Greek influence they rapidly adopted the latest ideas on urban development and spread them over a large part of the Italian peninsula. They were particularly concerned with the problems of drainage and irrigation and were capable of producing answers to the specific problems of their region. As in everything else, they acted as transmitters rather than creators. Their methods of construction remained fundamentally different from those of the Greeks, not only in the materials used but in their whole character. They never evolved the precise rules of design and proportion which dictate the progress of Greek architecture, except in a late period and then only under the influence of Hellenistic Greek theorizing. Their architecture was always soundly practical in approach, making use of the locally available materials and handling them with considerable skill.

On the hills and slopes that surrounded the cities, with a preference, perhaps, for the south and east sides, were the cemeteries. Most of them had been begun in Villanovan times as urnfields where the dead of the different tribal groups or settlements within the area were buried. The early development of these cemeteries and the evidence they give for the growth of the cities has already been discussed; here we are concerned only with the general appearance of these "cities of the dead" in the great period of Etruscan history, for in many ways they are the visible symbol of the economic and political strength of the city-states, as well as our chief source of knowledge for the life of the people. Caere's cemeteries completely surround the city, but are divided

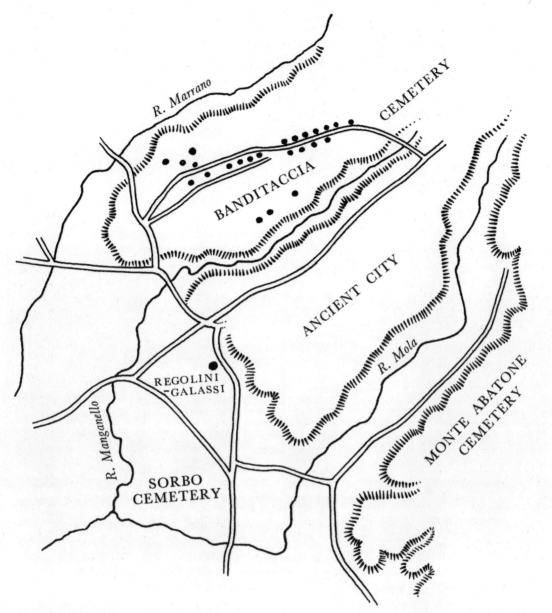

Plan of Caere and its cemeteries

from it by the valleys that isolate the site. Here one of the old Villanovan cemeteries was specially singled out for development in the later seventh century, superseding the chief Villanovan cemetery which lay nearest the city. This great cemetery, known as the Banditaccia, is distinguished by its series of massive earthen tumuli piled up on circular bases partly cut in the rock and partly built. The tumuli cover a number of separate chamber tombs, generally with a number of rooms. The interiors often imitate the construction and detail of the houses of the living, with the timber construction of the ceiling, and the detail of doors and windows carved in the solid stone; they were true houses of the dead, but built, unlike the houses of the living, in permanent

Interior of the Tomb of the Bulls, Tarquinia. The main picture shows the ambush of Troilus

materials to defy the ravages of time. The cemetery expanded rather haphazardly on either side of a main road at the eastern end of which several roads radiate; the massive early tumuli contrast strikingly with the modest burials around them, reflecting, as they do, a society with vast social differences. The later tumuli are more modest, and the chamber tombs of the fifth century are often quite simple and incorporated in a regular layout along straight streets.

The picture at Tarquinia, where the Monterozzi hill on the south was rapidly developed in the same period, is very similar. In the seventh century we find a few massive tumulus burials among the simple *fossa* or corridor tombs; these tumuli, either isolated or in groups, are obviously burials of nobles and powerful families. In the sixth century chamber tombs cut in the rock and perhaps covered by small tumuli became the rule; these tombs are more modest in size and many have richly painted interiors. There is no overall plan of development in the early period, but a haphazard growth utilizing the available space.

The importance of the cities of the dead for our knowledge of every aspect of Etruscan life cannot be overestimated; it is true to say that what we know of some Etruscan places comes almost entirely from their tombs. Here we can see the changing pattern of Etruscan society from its "heroic" age of kings, represented by the great tumuli of the seventh century, to the wealthy aristocracy of the sixth century and then the almost suburban middle class suggested by the cemeteries of Orvieto. We get glimpses of the progress of ideas in town-planning from the layout of some of the cemeteries and, more important, we can judge the skill of the Etruscans as builders which is scarcely hinted at in the remains of their cities. In the north, around Volterra and the middle valley of the Arno, some of the tombs show remarkable ability in the techniques of vaulting over spaces of circular plan by means of overlapping horizontal courses of stone. In the Tomba della Pietrera at Vetulonia the transition between a square chamber and a circular corbelled vault is made by means of pendentives of spherical triangular shape. It may be that the Etruscans invented this constructional feature which was to become so important an element of late Roman and Byzantine architecture, since it does not occur elsewhere as early as this.

Our knowledge of the smaller settlements within the city-states and of the pattern of settlement in general is so far inadequate. Ancient writers distinguish the different kinds of community as *urbes* (cities or towns), *castella* (forts) and *pagi* (villages). Although there was a tendency in the sixth century for the chief cities to grow at the expense of a number of small towns which had flourished in the early period, the territories throughout history contained a number of substantial town settlements which may have arisen for reasons of defence or as market centres. S. Giovenale on the edge of Tarquinia's territory was probably a typical market town originating in an Apennine village, later replaced by a Villanovan settlement on a slightly different site and finally becoming an "Etruscanized" town in the seventh century. S. Andrea, nearby, was probably a typical *castellum*, as was the town of Sutri on the edge of Etruscan territory where it commanded the gap between the two ranges of volcanic hills. Castellina was a frontier town on the north of the territory of Caere. The hinterland of Tarquinia, picturesque and wild, was thickly populated by small village communities usually sited in strong positions at the confluences of torrents and easily defended. Typical of this inland village settlement is the area between Lake Bolsena and the Lago di Vico, where there were many small villages to which the famous rock tombs of Bieda, Norchia and Castel d'Asso belong. The densest areas of settlement are in the south; in the northern territories the villages and towns were more widely spread. Sometimes impressive tombs are found in rural country districts, the burials, possibly, of the wealthy lords of the manor controlling considerable estates.

Chapter Seven

LIFE AND CUSTOMS

Many of the customs of the Etruscans seemed more or less strange to their neighbours, the Greeks and Romans, who constantly underline the differences between their own mentality and the Etruscan. But among our ancient writers really penetrating comment is rare, and much of what we hear is frankly scurrilous. A fourth-century Greek writer, Theopompus, whose work was widely read, produced some scandalous comment on their habits which scarcely bears examination – an unrelieved picture of decadence, wantonness, luxury and drunkenness. They shared this reputation with the Sybarites, and, indeed, with a number of colonial Greek cities, including the Cumaeans, in the eyes of other Greeks. Posidonius, the Stoic writer of the second century B.C., whom Diodorus Siculus used as a source, is a more accurate observer, contrasting their early valour with the luxury and softness of their latter days, which he attributes to the richness of their land. Modern critics have been scarcely more successful in their attempts to assess the Etruscan character. The prim Victorians would attribute the supposed moral and political decay to a perverse religion; the freethinkers praise an apparently uninhibited "joie de vivre". A female scholar once thought that the irrationality of the Etruscans was due to their favourable view of women; a male observer might be tempted to add their apparent lack of imagination to the same cause. Facile and often uninformed moralizing about the Etruscans seems to have been a failing common to both ancients and moderns, and if nowadays we are less prone to pass such judgments the problem of understanding their character and way of life remains a difficult one, for they seem to have been a curiously complex mixture of primitivism and culture, of wisdom and ignorance, of good and bad taste.

Etruria, in the three hundred years or so that concern us here, was a rapidly changing society and the basis of Posidonius' judgment that the manners and customs of the seventh-century Etruscans were far different from those of later days is completely valid. We are dealing with a people who eagerly accepted manners and modes of life from those with whom they came into contact and our problem is to assess how deep these foreign influences went, and what elements of character and habit continued to distinguish the Etruscans from other ancient peoples. The first society we can recognize as distinctly Etruscan is in many ways a primitive society where power rests with a warrior aristocracy, surrounded in life and in death by great pomp and ceremony. In such a society where man is surrounded by forces beyond his control or understanding, the ruler's power rests not only on military strength but on his ability to perform the precise ritual observances by which those forces may be propitiated. The complex rites, a mixture of sound practical sense and magic, however much they became modified and were transformed under Greek influence, remained the basis of Etruscan religious ritual. The king is both commander and chief priest and on his magical powers the safety of the community depends, and even in death these powers must be preserved and enhanced. Thus it is that an elaborate funerary ritual arises and in a time when men lived in modest and impermanent dwellings the tombs of the great are impressive monuments of permanent architecture in which they lie in all the splendid trappings of life.

In the great burials of the seventh century complex funerary ritual is clearly implied – the lying in state, the procession to the tomb or funeral pyre, the solemn committal of the body to the protection of the tomb. The funeral banquet is attested in early monuments, for example on a seventh-century cremation urn from Montescudaio near Volterra. To appease the spirits of the dead and give them strength in the after-life, funeral games were celebrated, games in which, perhaps, human sacrifice was originally involved. In the later Etruscan tomb-paintings, as we shall see, there is evidence for the survival of games in connection with funerals which involved the death or maiming of the participants; the origins of such games may lie in the earliest period of Etruscan civilization. The armed dance of the warriors of the tribe is certainly an early feature of funerary ritual. A special game, also of early origins, was the so-called Game of Troy, a complicated military ride which was later performed at the *Ludi Magni* in Rome and is vividly described by Virgil in the fifth book of the *Aeneid*; it seems to be depicted on a seventh-century painted jug found in a chamber tomb at Tragliatella near Bracciano where two horsemen and seven armed dancers are shown issuing from a kind of labyrinth in which is written the word *truia*. These may not be funeral games; they could be ceremonies performed by the young men of the tribal aristocracy as part of their military education and ceremony. Armed dances are shown on other early Etruscan monuments.

In the early Etruscan society women already have a place of importance and share in the magical ritual that surrounds the rulers. In the main chamber of the great Regolini-Galassi tumulus lies the princess in her gilded dress and gold pectoral with her throne and many other precious belongings about her. Legends bear out this picture of the status of women and of their influence in public affairs, and while it would be wrong to think of Etruria as in any sense a matriarchal society it is clear that the Etruscan woman occupied a very important place in the closely-knit family unit which seems to have been the basis of Etruscan life. Tanaquil, the wife of old Tarquin of Rome, is perhaps the model of everything a good Etruscan wife should be, encouraging her husband in his political ambitions and at the same time skilled in the domestic arts. To this she added education, being well versed in mathematics and medicine. The freedom of the Etruscan women was obviously, as the ancients often observed, much greater than in most contemporary Mediterranean societies.

The material and cultural advance of primitive Etruscan society depended, as we have seen, upon the stimulus of their contacts with the Greeks and other peoples who came to trade with them. In a society such as this the exotic soon acquires supernatural powers, and this fact does much to explain the remarkable receptiveness of early Etruria to all kinds of foreign influences. The old Villanovan artistic tradition is non-representational, symbolic, lacking in visual imagination; now a flood of representa-tional art of Greek and oriental inspiration comes into the country and is given a new significance. The women who had worn rich jewellery of bronze – hair spirals, earrings, fibulae – now eagerly collect oriental jewellery to which they attribute magical powers. The Phoenician symbols of sun and moon and the Egyptian scarab acquire a new significance and meaning; ritual vessels, based on eastern models, accompany the dead. These new influences go much deeper than mere imitation of something strange. The oriental world of weird and fantastic animals – lions, panthers, sphinxes (plate 6) – acquires the power to protect the tombs of the dead, and soon the divine powers begin to be conceived in human form, according to the canons of Greek or oriental art. Divine figures of oriental form stand guard over the tombs.

The "orientalizing" period of the seventh century was clearly a vital step in the development of Etruscan culture. However these oriental objects reached Etruria, there can be no doubt that they produced a genuine and creative response and penetrated deep into the whole fabric of Etruscan life. It was a response far more vital than that which the severity and restraint of early Greek art could have produced in this primitive people. Ostentatious and vulgar much of the art of the period may be, but it has the honesty of an uninhibited love of luxury and wealth. Etruscan ladies began to wear their hair in oriental fashion, to give up the severe dress in favour of patterned oriental draperies and to wear jewellery of gold and silver of fantastic elaboration (plate 2). But these are fashions, and fashions change. It is the elements of higher culture which have the more lasting effect – a half-understood mythology is adapted to local beliefs, an alphabet is learnt to write their language, foreign divinities are adopted to give form to insubstantial but powerful divine forces.

The most obvious proof of cultural advance in this period is certainly the adoption of writing, somewhere about the middle of the seventh century B.C. In one of the tombs of the Circolo degli Avori at Marsiliana there was found an ivory writing tablet on the edge of which is engraved a specimen alphabet, derived like all ancient alphabets from the Phoenician but in a form which shows that it came through a Greek source. At first, no doubt, the knowledge of writing was confined to a few; among primitive people writing is power, as Livy reminds us when he says of King Evander that "he was revered for his invention of letters – a strange and wonderful thing to the rude, uncultivated men amongst whom he dwelt". Indeed the alphabet acquired and maintained something of a magical significance, so that it survived in its original form long after several of the letters had gone out of use in practical writing. The spread of writing in Etruria was rapid and in the later seventh century there are many inscriptions on pottery in the Etruscan language from widely scattered parts of Etruria. These inscriptions sometimes occupy a prominent position on the pots, forming the principal decorative motif; some of them are quite lengthy and show the rapid development of formal expression in the Etruscan language. Through Etruria the knowledge of writing reached the peoples of central Italy and spread as far as the sub-Alpine regions of the north; its propagation was among the greatest contributions that the Etruscans made to the civilization of Italy.

From the sixth century the Greeks exerted a dominating influence on every branch of Etruscan life, and one problem is to assess the depth of this influence. No doubt it varied considerably from place to place. At Caere and Tarquinia a Greek could almost feel at home. Caere had a Greek name, Agylla, a treasury at Delphi whose oracle it

 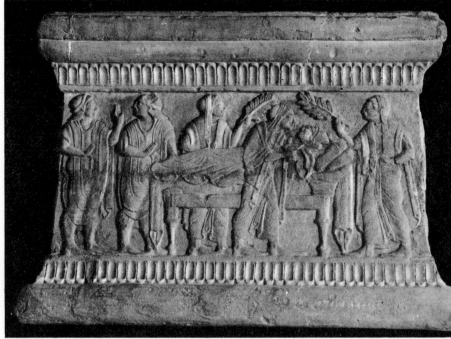

Left. Clay cremation urn from Montescudaio. A funerary banquet is depicted on the lid. *Right*. Stone grave *cippus* from Clusium, showing the laying out of the dead

frequently consulted, a notable Greek element in its population; sixth-century Clusium must have been a very different place, preserving much more of its old way of life. From the middle of the century we begin to get a vivid picture of the Etruscans through a particularly expressive series of tomb-monuments, especially the paintings in the interior of tomb chambers at Tarquinia and elsewhere, which do much to recreate the environment of life. We are now in the full flood of Greek influence, when contacts with the Greeks were closest, with Sybaris in the south and the cities of Campania, and when Greek trade was beginning to flow through Spina and the other stations at the head of the Adriatic. The paintings show us many facets of Etruscan daily life, how they dined, what they wore, what their pastimes were, something of their religious beliefs. Some caution is needed in the use of the evidence. When we look, for example, at a banquet scene painted on a tomb wall we cannot always be sure of its precise significance, whether we are looking at a funerary banquet, a picture of real life, or an ideal creation of a life beyond the tomb. Much of the symbolism of the pictures is not clearly understood, but generally we are in little doubt that we are seeing the Etruscans as they were or as they wished to be.

Of their funerary rites and practices we can tell a good deal. On some of the carved urns and *cippi* from Clusium there are scenes showing several preparatory rites – the women of the family selecting the robes and draperies in which the dead will be laid out, the laying out of the body with scented oils poured upon it, mourning scenes where the body is shown covered in rich drapery while the women mourners beat their breasts

83

and the men hold their hands to their heads. Other scenes show the men preparing for the games and spectacles which will accompany the funerary rites. Then follows the procession to the tomb, the women covering their heads, the men in short tunics and cloaks; the dead are taken to their resting place in a carriage on which the funeral couch is set. In the family tombs of Caere we see the carved beds and sarcophagi in which they lay, a couch for the men and a shallow gable-ended sarcophagus for the women. But these details, of course, varied very much from place to place. At Clusium, where the rite of cremation long prevailed, a mask is placed over the face when the dead man is taken to his funeral pyre, and his ashes are placed in a vase with the lid in the form of a human head or in a prepared cavity in the upper part of a sculptured figure or in an urn decorated with reliefs.

Many of these funerary ceremonies go back to the earliest traditions of Etruria. Sometimes we see scenes of special significance, not always easy to understand. In the Tomb of the Funerary Couch at Tarquinia, in a scene which appears to be taking place

Bronze death masks from Clusium

within a large pavilion, homage is paid to a great couch on which are white cones and a wreath. A special moment in the rites seems to be shown on the end wall of the Tomb of the Augurs which contains a representation of the door of the tomb flanked by two grave, bearded men in attitudes of grief. They wear typical Etruscan outdoor dress of the period – long tunic, a cloak held on both shoulders, and the characteristic Etruscan shoes with upturned pointed toes. In the Tomba del Morto the dead is shown laid out beneath a rich scarlet cloth; the head is exposed and wears the conical cap, the *tutulus*, which was popular among women at the time and is an eastern form. Underlying most of these funerary rites is the belief that the dead continue to live in the protection of the tomb. New ideas, derived perhaps from the Greeks, were beginning to make themselves felt and in the end transformed the funerary symbolism of the Etruscans, but most of the evidence for a new imagery of death is late. A few early monuments show scenes where the dead person appears to be riding to the underworld or is accompanied by winged demons, but the representations of the underworld and of those

End wall of the Tomb of the Augurs, Tarquinia, showing bearded men in attitudes of grief

Banquet scene in the Tomb of the Leopards, Tarquinia

monstrously frightening guides of the soul – Charon and Tuchulcha – are not earlier than the fourth century. Greek ideas, derived from Orphism and Pythagoreanism, lie at the base of much of this, and were later incorporated in the Etruscan Books of the Dead, the *Libri Acheruntici*.

The commonest scene in the paintings of Tarquinia is the banquet. There is no doubt that an actual banquet in honour of the dead formed part of the Etruscan funerary rites, but whatever theory we hold to about the significance of the banquet scene in Etruscan tomb-paintings – whether it depicts the funerary banquet, or the life of the blessed, or merely serves to cheer the dead – there is little doubt that the artists' inspiration comes from scenes of life in which they had participated. We cannot doubt this when we look at the charming domestic scene on the Tomb of the Painted Vases at Tarquinia where husband and wife share wine together and their two little children sit by them, the boy on the girl's knee, while a dog waits expectantly at the foot of their banquet couch. We are even introduced to the kitchen where the slaves, to a musical accompaniment, are shown preparing the massive meals that the Etruscans are reputed to have eaten twice a day. The banquet scene may be quite simple, just two people on a couch with attendants – children, musicians and slaves; three couches is the normal rule and the banquet is always accompanied by music and dance. The banqueters recline in pairs, often husband and wife together, on handsome couches with richly embroidered covers, the women in their finest dresses, the men generally semi-nude in the fashion adopted from the Greeks. In the second half of the sixth century they dined reclining, another Greek habit; earlier they probably sat, and sometimes the women are shown seated in the company of reclining men.

These gay and colourful paintings are a vivid recreation of the domestic life of the

wealthy Etruscans of the period. We see the richness of the interior furnishings –
couches with ornamental legs with large mattresses put over them and ample cushions
with embroidered covers, rectangular and round tables on which the food and drink
are set before the diners, chairs like thrones with barrel-shaped bottom and rounded
back, stools and footrests. There are candelabra of a type peculiar to Etruria where
candles were used for interior lighting in preference to the olive-oil lamp, because olive-
oil was always an expensive and largely imported commodity. The interiors of Etruscan
houses were noted for the richness of their furnishings and even the Greeks granted the
Etruscan skill in the manufacture of high-class domestic fittings. "Anything of bronze
for the decoration of the house," says an Athenian, Kritias the tyrant, son of Kallikrates,
"is best if it is Etruscan."

The banquet is always a scene of music and dancing. The dancers are domestic
slaves, and in the Tomb of the Inscriptions at Tarquinia they are named and presum-
able represent real people, not ideal figures. The pictures of dancers are among the
liveliest that have come down to us. In the Tomb of the Lionesses at Tarquinia a
magnificently dressed woman dancer wears an orange-red *tutulus* dotted with embroidered flowers, a long belted dress to match her head-dress, and a brightly coloured
mantle of blue with a red lining. Her shoes have pointed toes and she wears ear-rings.
Fashions of female dress were changing and Greek Ionic dress beginning to predomi-
nate, but there are traces of earlier fashions in the cut of some of them and in the way
they are worn. The women prefer to wear their cloaks over both shoulders as they did
in the seventh century and their footwear remains distinctive, though they have given
up their old hairstyles in favour of Greek fashions. They love dresses richly embroidered
with floral patterns which in Greece are worn only by the *hetaira*. Their jewellery is still
rich, but less ostentatious and more Greek in taste. The male dancers are simply dressed
with embroidered cloaks generally draped over both shoulders. The men and women
dance with expansive gestures of the hand, to the music of the pipe with the girls playing
castanets and jingling bells. A man and woman in the scene dance together to the pipe
and the lyre. Everything in Etruria, we are told, needed background music, so music
cheers the dead and placates the spirits of the underworld just as it inspires the slave
in his kitchen and the master at his banquet. The instruments they play are mostly
Greek with a few special Etruscan wind instruments; castanets beat the rhythm.

The second most common subject of the Etruscan tomb-paintings is games and
sports. If the banquet is not always a funerary banquet, the games presumably are not
always funerary games. We know, in fact, that the Etruscans celebrated games on
many occasions. The state calendar was full of religious festivals, many of which were
accompanied by games of various kinds, and games were an essential part of the rites
associated with military triumph which the Romans took over from the Etruscans. One
of the festivals of Caere was Greek-inspired. We are told that after the Battle of Alalia
when the Caeretans had massacred the Phocaean survivors they suffered a plague and
consulted Delphi where the Oracle instructed them to establish annual ceremonies
including games and horse-racing in honour of the Phocaeans. But there was also a long
tradition of games in honour of the dead, as we have already seen; these developed a
strongly Hellenic taste in the sixth century and most of the Greek sports were performed.
A black-figure vase by an artist known as the Micali painter, the best of the black-figure

painters of Vulci in the late sixth century, gives us the varied repertory of an Etruscan sports meeting, including two massive boxers fighting to the strains of the flute, a pentathlon, an armed dance, a chariot race with two chariots round the post neck and neck and a dog adding to the excitement, and what looks like a satyr dance. The wonderfully evocative scene of the Tomb of the Bigas shows the temporary stands for the spectators watching the games; the wooden superstructure is loosely draped with cloth to keep off the sun from the spectators who are seated to watch the festivities. Below the platform of the seats are figures who are usually interpreted as slaves or the common people.

Apart from games of Greek inspiration, there are one or two examples of cruel blood sports which may be survivals of rites of human sacrifice at the graves of early rulers. The chief evidence is the famous scene from the Tomb of the Augurs at Tarquinia where a masked man is setting a fierce dog which he holds on a leash against another man who is armed with a club but severely handicapped by having his head in a bag. The dog has already taken a savage bite into his victim's thigh. The masked figure is named as *Phersu* in the accompanying inscription, and he appears again in the recently discovered Tomb of the Olympic Games at Tarquinia. The scenes depict an organized blood sport of some kind which has no Hellenic connections; we are reminded that one tradition, at least, attributed the origin of the Roman gladiatorial games to the Etruscans, and that the Roman word for a trainer of gladiators – *lanista* – appears to be Etruscan. But nothing suggests that these cruel sports were the main attraction of the Etruscan games. Most of the Etruscan games are Greek in origin, and critics of the Etruscans have usually drawn attention to what they believe to be a fundamental difference in attitude: that these are not noble sports but simply a form of light entertainment performed largely by professionals, generally slaves. Athletics may not have been, as they were in Greece, an expression of national character, but we have no real reason to assume that the aristocratic youth of Etruria did not enjoy these activities for very much the same reasons as the Greeks. They competed, like the Greeks, for simple prizes; in a funerary relief from Clusium in Palermo, the judges are shown seated on a raised dais with the prizes, a number of wineskins, between them. The participants here are a warrior, a dancer, a flautist, an athlete with a discus and a spear. Another *cippus* shows a running-race with three large pots as prizes. Prizes are sometimes helmets and vessels of bronze or precious metal. The referees kept a close watch on the competitors, especially in the form of wrestling known to the Greeks as the *pankration*; in one scene a referee is shown armed with a whip and ready to step in and deal with any breach of the rules.

Every phase of the exciting sport of chariot-racing is shown on the monuments. The favourite vehicle in Etruria was the light two-horse chariot, the *biga*; the charioteer generally wore the short, belted *chiton*, which was also popular in Ionia, and went bareheaded like the Greeks, though sometimes he wore the *tutulus*. Tradition has it that the Etruscan king of Rome, Tarquin the Elder, built the Circus Maximus in Rome for chariot racing and boxing, and brought the first performers from Etruria. The preparations for the race were followed by a parade of the competing chariots around the circus. Tree-trunks apparently served as turning posts at either end. The artists of the tomb-paintings sometimes conjure up a wonderful picture of the excite-

Two scenes from a black-figure vase found at Vulci. Two boxers fighting to an accompaniment of music (*top*); and athletes, with chariot horses at the turning post

Above top. Spectators watching a parade of chariots, from the Tomb of the Bigas, Tarquinia.
Above. Scene of fighting, in the Tomb of the Augurs, Tarquinia

Chariot at speed, from the Tomb of the Olympic Games, Tarquinia

ment of the race. In one painted tomb at Clusium, a charioteer at speed is suddenly thrown from his chariot, and a remarkable scene is painted on the walls of the Tomb of the Olympic Games at Tarquinia, the work of one of the most brilliant Etruscan tomb-painters (plate 11). The charioteers wear short blue tunics and one has what looks like a crash-helmet. Four chariots are involved, and the last episode depicts a dramatic pile-up of two of them, a scene observed with horror by three woman spectators. On a fine Etruscan black-figure vase from Vulci in Berlin a race of three-horse chariots is depicted at the moment when the trumpeters are sounding the last turn; the wild excitement of the moment is vividly captured by the painter.

Although it is clear that Greek influence penetrated every part of Etruscan life in the course of the sixth and fifth centuries, it is a more subtle problem to assess how much of the higher culture of the Greeks was truly assimilated by the Etruscans of the day. In these centuries the Greeks achieved epic and lyric poetry, drama, history and oratory, won renown in philosophy, science and medicine, and developed new ideas of constitutional government. How much of all this was understood in Etruria? The question is one which it is difficult, almost impossible, at present, to answer, but it is becoming increasingly apparent that in the southern cities, at least, the degree of "hellenization" must have been very considerable. It was argued recently by a French scholar that when the Roman aristocracy sent their sons, as we know they did in the fourth century B.C., to be educated at Caere, they did so because Caere was a city where Greek culture flourished, where the educated were probably bilingual in Greek and Etruscan, and where Greek

91

literature was known and taught. One would hesitate to go the whole way with this view, because even at Caere Greek inscriptions are comparatively rare, though Greek loan-words in the Etruscan language include not only the things one would expect, like the names of vases (e.g. *pruchum*, from πρόχους, a jug), but at least a few words derived from Greek politics, science and thought. Clearly we shall not know the answer to this problem until the language is fully understood but several significant equations of Greek and Etruscan words are instructive: *purthne*, an Etruscan official, and πρυτάνις, is one such.

The wealthy Etruscans of the fifth century, with, at least, an appreciable Greek element in the population of their cities and close ties of guest-friendship with other Greek cities, obviously did much more than imitate the dress, the banqueting habits, and the games of the Greeks. It is clear, for example, that the rites of the Etruscan marriage ceremony were closely related to those of the Greeks. On a sard intaglio in Boston one side shows the bride and groom sitting in a two-wheeled carriage drawn by four horses and accompanied by attendants; the procession is led by a woman playing a double pipe. On the other side is shown the bridegroom's house with a gabled front where a woman is preparing the marriage bed, and a bearded man and a woman, the bridegroom's parents, are waiting to welcome the couple. This is a slice of life and closely related to Greek practice. The Etruscan girl would probably dress in the Greek manner, wear Greek jewellery and live in a household where Greek objects were ardently collected. She might be the daughter of a wealthy merchant such as the man who was buried in the recently discovered Tomb of the Ship at Tarquinia; on the walls of his tomb we see depicted a fine square-rigged merchant vessel of Greek build and a large collection of Greek vases in which he obviously took pride. She would certainly be well acquainted with Greek heroic legend which formed the chief subject-matter for these vases. On her mirror might be depicted a scene from Homer's *Iliad* with the names of the heroes written in their Etruscan equivalents. She knew the Greek gods and their mythology. She might have visited Greek cities in the south of Italy and certainly knew many Greeks.

New ideas, religious beliefs and political conceptions must have followed in such an atmosphere, and their influence can be seen everywhere, not least in the sphere where the Etruscans show their greatest independence of thought, namely the sphere of religion. The basis of Etruscan religion was, as we have seen, the careful observation of a prescribed ritual which traditionally was revealed to the *lucumones* by a number of divine or semi-divine beings. These were complex rites compounded of theology, astrology, and sound practical knowledge which were eventually written down in the famous Etruscan books – the books of haruspicy or the examination of entrails, the books of lightning, and the books of ritual which contained the prescriptions of law and custom relating to many aspects of life. Other books, the *Libri Acheruntici*, or Books of the Dead, revealed the secrets of the underworld. The body of this holy writ had a powerful influence in later times, and much of it was already written down in the fifth century B.C. In early days, knowledge of the ritual was confined to the rulers and a narrow priestly class of *augurs* and *haruspices*; they alone understood how to examine the livers of sacrificial animals and establish what the omens were, they alone could set out the sacred area, the templum, which corresponded with the divisions of the

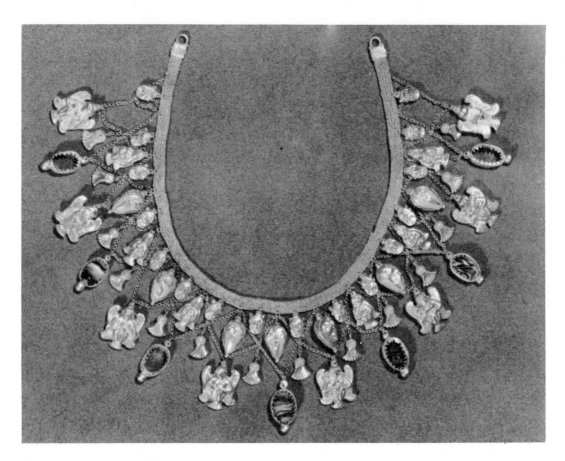

Etruscan gold necklace. About 500 B.C.

heavens, and knew who were the divinities that hurled thunderbolts, where they hurled them from and what exactly they meant. The priestly education required a sound practical knowledge of geometry and astronomy, and the *augurs* and *haruspices* were men of some learning with considerable influence in the political and social life of the cities.

Much of this body of ritual is original to the Etruscans, or, at least, we cannot establish where they got it from. Orientals, including Babylonians and Hittites, and some Greeks, practised haruspicy but we cannot say from what source it came to the Etruscans or how it developed from the earliest period. The rites differed very much from place to place, as Cicero specifically tells us. Etruscan haruspicy as we know it from late documents is a highly complex rite compounded of theology and astrology; our chief evidence is a bronze liver of the third century B.C. found at Piacenza which is divided into sixteen main parts, each belonging to a god and to various subordinate divinities. It is a sort of text book for the haruspex who, with its aid, would be able to judge from the conditions of the various parts of the sacrificial liver which gods were favourable and which were not. Other elements of Etruscan religious ritual were widespread in the ancient world: lightning and thunder were everywhere held to be signs of the will of the gods and, as Cicero observes, there was no shortage of work for the

The bronze augural liver from Piacenza

Etruscan priests because of the heaviness of the atmosphere. The early doctrines of thunderbolts were probably transformed under Greek and Oriental influence. In origin, much Etruscan ritual deals with propitiation of unseen powers who have no clear substantial form; the early religious experience of the Etruscans is not concerned with theology and indeed seems to lack any visual imagination. When their divinities take visible shape it is under Greek and oriental influence; the gods begin to be conceived in human form, temples are built to give them a worthy home on earth, sacrifice is made to them as individuals. In their sanctuaries there are altars for sacrifice, in their temples cult-statues. One of the earliest Etruscan sacrificial scenes appears on a grave-relief from Clusium; on a lighted altar stands an incense burner and three attendants are bringing a bull for sacrifice. Three other attendants, wearing short tunics and conical hats, stand waiting with knives in their right hands and make gestures of worship with their left hands. Gods in human form had certainly appeared as early as the beginning of the sixth century, as protectors of the dead and soon as objects of worship; the state calendars were soon filled with religious festivals in honour of various divinities, and the year, originally of ten months and later of twelve, was divided into lucky and unlucky days, time being calculated in accordance with the phases of the moon.

A large measure of Etruscan theology is clearly derived from Greek and oriental sources within the period we are dealing with here. At first sight one would be inclined to think that the Greek gods, who dominate the art of the area, were simply taken over in full by the Etruscans. Such a conclusion would be false and misleading. To worshippers with their heads full of Greek legend and mythology, it was easy to identify their own divinities with those of the Greeks, and their lack of a speculative theology made them particularly susceptible to this kind of identification. Thus Tinia, their chief god, was apparently identified with Zeus, Menrva with Athena, and their outward appearance in art is identical. But it must be remembered that a god of very different functions can be identified with an invading divinity, as happened very often in the Greco-Roman Near East, and yet retain his own special character in the minds of his devotees. Varro says that the supreme god of the Etruscans was the sky and that the others had an astral character; Martianus Capella, a Byzantine writer, tells us of a hierarchy of gods which is scarcely hinted at in Etruscan art. The bronze liver of Piacenza contains the names of a great mass of minor divinities who are unknown to us. Vortumnus or Voltumna, the god of Volsinii, is never represented in art, so far as we know, and there are many other local divinities who are scarcely more than names.

The whole subject of Etruscan religion illustrates most clearly the interaction of Etruscan and Greek thought and beliefs. We find a body of ritual observance largely peculiar to the people overlaid with a theology and other elements quite clearly derived from Greece. But not even the derivative elements are necessarily taken over in their pure form, nor do they always satisfy Etruscan religious thinking. Apollo may be adopted in pure Greek form but Aphrodite is identified with Turan, a goddess of Etruscan name and function. Mars is identified with Ares but retains his Etruscan attributes. The mythology of Hercules, one of the most popular Greek divinities in Etruria, differs from the canonical form it has in the Greek world. At the same time foreign gods are worshipped in their pure forms in Etruscan cities – Hera in the Manganello temple at Caere and the Phoenician Astarte in Pyrgi, as the gold plaques recently found there reveal. When the long religious texts which have come down to us, the Capua tile and the rest, can be read in detail we shall, no doubt, understand these interactions of different religious beliefs; until then we must admit that much is only half-understood.

Closely linked with the question of religion is that of law. It was not until 450 B.C., half a century after the establishment of the Republic, that the Romans drew up their first code of law, the Twelve Tables, which made public a body of custom-law, the knowledge of which had been confined to the priesthood. By tradition they consulted Athens and there does seem to be a Greek influence in the enactments of the Tables. In the early Etruscan communities the priestly class must similarly have been the main repository of custom-law, and there is evidence for the growth of a religious law common to all the peoples of Etruria. But as the early states developed from kingship to aristocracy, an increasing secularization of law must have followed and the Etruscan states were far more open to Greek influence than Rome. We may suppose that very much the same process happened in many Etruscan cities as happened in Rome in the fifth century.

The Etruscans of the sixth and fifth centuries were widely literate, as we know from extensive finds of inscriptions on all kinds of objects; but how far did they develop a literature of their own? The question has been much argued about. Some think that the Etruscans had their own written versions of Greek epics which often differed from the Greek; others point to misinterpretations of Greek mythology and burlesqued versions of Greek stories which seem to argue against a literary appreciation of the Greek tradition and an Etruscan epic literature. The chief use of the written language was clearly to preserve the tradition of religious ritual and practice which was, to some extent, common to all the states of Etruria. Two of the longest early inscriptions, the Magliano lead plaque and the Capua tile of the sixth century B.C., are documents containing religious prescriptions of various kinds. There is some evidence for the use of verse composition in these texts since everything didactic gains from such a presentation.

It is highly unlikely that this was the only native literature in ancient Etruria. One can hardly doubt that heroic lays were sung on great occasions to celebrate great deeds, and that some of these were preserved in written form in the annals of the great families. The stories depicted on the walls of the François Tomb approach the proportions of an epic and are paralleled by scenes from the Trojan saga which were widely current in Etruria in the fifth century when the tradition of the Trojan foundation of several Etruscan cities was generally accepted. Verse of some sort was no doubt sung, and there may have been acting of a kind, at triumphal ceremonies, marriages, funerals, harvest festivals and the like; much of it was probably improvised and of a scurrilous nature and we have no evidence that poetry and drama became established art forms in Etruria. It may be that the Etruscans wrote their own versions of Greek mythology, but there is no hint that scenic performances in the Greek manner took place in any of their cities. In the *locus classicus* on the origin of Roman drama, Livy tells us that in 364 B.C. Etruscan dancers to the flute were summoned to Rome when stage performances were added to the Circus games, but it was the Roman youth who added their scurrilous verses with music accompaniment, song and gesture, and so created the art-form known as the *satura* from which the Roman drama had its origins. While it is quite possible that Greek epic and dramatic poetry were known and read, there is no suggestion that these writings produced a creative response in any of the Etruscan cities.

Writing must have been extensively used in everyday affairs – in business transactions, administration, legal documents; and, if prose history was not written until a much later period, many historical documents, including priestly records, treaties, laws and the like must have survived from quite an early period. Many of these records are incorporated in our later historical sources. Commemorative statues of great men which were set up in the public places of the cities were probably accompanied by inscriptions extolling their deeds. In the fifth century when aristocratic government had superseded the rule of kings, the art of oratory must have been developed in many of the cities, and one cannot rule out the possibility that famous speeches were recorded. It is almost certain that when our Etruscan texts are finally translated they will reveal the existence of a fairly extensive literature of different kinds, indebted in many ways to Greek sources of inspiration.

And what of science and philosophy? Everything we know about the Etruscans suggests that they had a fundamentally different conception of the world and of the destiny of man from that of their Greek contemporaries. Seneca gives us a revealing comment on the attitude of the Etruscans to natural phenomena when he points out the difference between the Etruscan and Roman view of lightning, the former supernatural, the latter giving it a rational explanation. On the other hand what we learn of the Etruscans from their surviving remains reveals that at the basis of their life is a

Plate 9. *Bucchero* jug with spout in the form of a bull's head; *bucchero* with relief decoration is characteristic of the sixth century B.C. From Chiusi. (Museo Archeologico, Florence)
Overleaf Plate 10. Wall painting of a male and a female dancer from the Tomb of the Triclinium, Tarquinia. About 470 B.C.

sound practical knowledge and experience which was quick to recognize the value of much of what Greek rationalism had to teach. They were able land surveyors and adopted Greek methods of planning; their theology has a background of practical mathematics. In medicine they were celebrated, at least, for their knowledge of herbal cures but they probably obtained a good deal of medical theory from the school of Croton which was most influential in the late sixth century when the Etruscans occupied Campania and were in close contact with the southern Greek cities. In dentistry there can be no doubt of their skill. They could bridge and crown a tooth with a technique which impresses modern dentists. Two examples of Etruscan bridging may be seen in the Liverpool Museum, one showing a bridge between two sound teeth, originally containing two false ones; the examples are undated but there is good reason to think that the technique goes back to an early period. There can be little doubt that many facets of Greek practical science were eagerly adopted by Etruria and, indeed, that the Etruscans themselves had contributions of their own to make.

Greek speculative philosophy and Greek ethics must have made far less impact in Etruria. Greek humanism could never have put down deep roots in the atmosphere of Etruscan religion, and only a few Etruscans can have attempted to understand the philosophical systems of the Greek thinkers. But, oddly enough, we hear that one of the first pupils of the philosopher Pythagoras of Rhegium was a certain Tyrsenos or Tyrsenis who ought to be an Etruscan. He, or she, must have been exceptional for nothing is more sure than the Etruscans' failure to understand the humanistic ideals of Greek culture. This is clear in their attitude to Greek art, which will be considered in more detail in the next chapter. The rich Etruscan collected Greek objets d'art; he needed them around him and vastly admired them, but he never seems to have comprehended the ideals that lie behind much of the Greek artistic output or its seriousness of purpose. The discipline and ordered development of Greek architecture, the ideal form and proportion of Greek statues and their all-pervading humanism were beyond his comprehension. There is a moment in Etruscan art, in the early fifth century, when it seems that Greek ideals are beginning to be fully understood, but it is short-lived, and thereafter while the Greeks developed their classical ideal, Etruscan art shows a lack of stylistic continuity which severs it completely from the creative achievement of the "classical revolution"

The time is significant. It is early Etruscan civilization down to about 480 B.C., when relations with the Greeks were closest, that achieved most as an intermediary of Greek culture in Italy and it is the early culture of Greece, not the developed classical civilization, that made the greatest impact. Contacts which were close and direct had brought about an astonishing transformation in the archaic civilization of Etruria. But just when the Greeks were to achieve most in every branch of science, literature and art, the most direct and fruitful links between Etruria and Greece were broken and Etruria, at enmity with the Greek colonies, may have fallen back on a deliberate antipathy to Greek culture. You would not, then, find a Greek theatre or hear a Greek play at Caere or Tarquinia, nor a Greek philosopher disputing with his pupils on political theory. But it might have happened and perhaps nearly did. There was a moment at the end of the sixth century when the penetration of Greek ideas was so deep that it would almost seem inevitable. But history was against it and at this moment relations with the Greeks

Plate 11. Wall painting of a chariot race from the Tomb of the Olympic Games, Tarquinia. About 520 B.C.
Plate 12. Wall painting of a reclining banqueter holding a drinking-cup in his left hand and an egg in his right. From the Tomb of the Lionesses, Tarquinia. About 510 B.C.

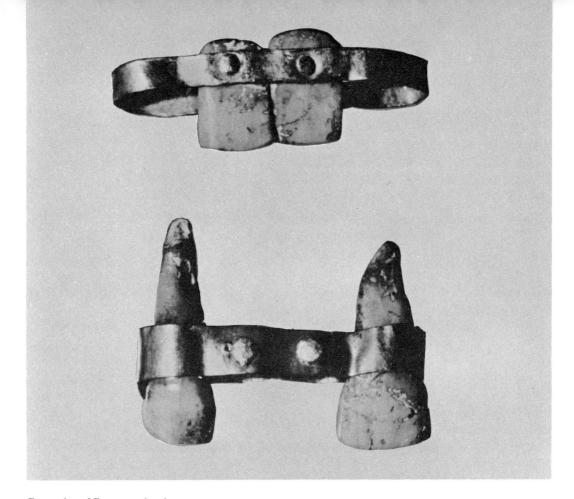

Examples of Etruscan dentistry

declined. Cumae was alienated, Syracuse an implacable enemy; the flow of Greek immigrants into what were becoming increasingly sympathetic communities was broken. A flourishing trade through the northern colonies, which went on for almost a century, was no substitute for the direct contacts that had influenced every branch of Etruscan life.

Chapter Eight

ART

The Etruscan had many uses for art, and if he was not a connoisseur, he liked to have art and good craftsmanship around him in everyday life; he was an ardent collector of *objets d'art*, both for show and for use. He recognized, if not with the clear understanding of the Greeks, the nobler purpose of art as an expression of human experience, and the religious and funerary art of the Etruscans often reveals a genuine independence of thought and feeling. It throws up, rarely perhaps, a real artistic personality, like the painter of the immensely dramatic chariot scenes in the Tomb of the Olympic Games (plate 11), or a work of art of outstanding delicacy or one of massive strength like the Apollo of Veii. But Etruscan art, however creative, is essentially a response to external stimuli and lacks a consistent internal development; it lies outside the main stream of European art and has no great influence upon it. To understand Etruscan art fully requires an intimate knowledge both of classical art in general and of the independent origins of much of its inspiration.

It should be said at the beginning that there is still much to be learnt about the bare bones of Etruscan art; we need to be able to distinguish the various schools and draw clear lines between what may be called metropolitan and provincial Etruscan work. Our material is full of apparent contradictions. The refined "hellenising" Etruscan style of the southern cities has to be set against, say, the local style of Perugia in the fifth century B.C., represented by figures of warriors and gods with spindly limbs, elongated bodies and little heads, owing little except their poses to Greek inspiration. Perugia, admittedly, is on the fringe of Etruria, perhaps not fully Etruscan till the late fifth century, but at Clusium, in a period when the coastal cities closely follow the traditions of archaic Greek art, the local funerary masks and canopic urns seem to reveal a fundamentally different approach to the rendering of human figures – inorganic and emphasising expressive details. To many students such work demonstrates a positive and powerful anti-classical taste in the artistic temperament of central Italy – the opposite pole of a duality which created the Apollo of Veii or the figures on Caeretan clay sarcophagi. They see it as a different artistic vision, expressing itself in a tendency to inorganic and superficial treatment of form, in emphasis on expressive details. These, at any rate, are factors that must be kept in mind when comparing an Etruscan and a Greek work; and, indeed, in considering the whole history of art in Etruria from the earliest times.

The Villanovan art and craftsmanship of the eighth century B.C., the pure Villanovan of Archaic I in Etruria, are expressed in the decoration of pottery and bronzes, made for various practical and ritual uses. It is fundamentally a non-representational art using a fairly wide repertory of abstract geometric patterns, independent, so far as we can

Left. Bronze figure of a warrior, from the Perugia district. Fifth century B.C. *Right.* Terracotta cinerary urn, from Clusium

Terracotta sarcophagus from Caere. About 500 B.C.

tell, of the contemporary Greek geometric tradition, though many of the patterns – the stepped maeander, the broken maeander, the chevron, the herringbone, the swastika panels – are common to both. Incision is the chief method of decoration on the pottery vessels, among which the biconical cinerary urn is the most characteristic shape; the incisions were often filled with chalk to throw up the lines of the patterns. Bronze objects were also incised with geometric patterns of various kinds. Then in the later eighth century, the period of Archaic II, a transformation begins. Zoomorphic elements, in severely schematic form, begin to appear, like the heraldic birds incorporated into the superb engraved design of a bronze belt from Bologna. A distinctive funerary art, springing from a developing sense of personality, now makes its appearance. The idea that the urn not only protects but in some way represents the dead lies at the root of this development. The urns of the south are covered with helmet-lids, and a cap-like bronze helmet found in a cemetery at Tarquinia and now in the Archaeological Museum at Florence is decorated with a schematic face. At Clusium a bronze mask is often attached to the urn, and later the urn takes on a simplified human form and is fitted with a lid in the form of a human head.

Although the character of this early funerary art varies from place to place, everywhere an increasing self-awareness is expressed in the representation of human and animal forms. The chief inspiration is the geometric art of Greece which has by now established clear-cut formulae for human and animal figures. In the later phase of Archaic II in which bronze becomes much more common, the taste for figured work is

106

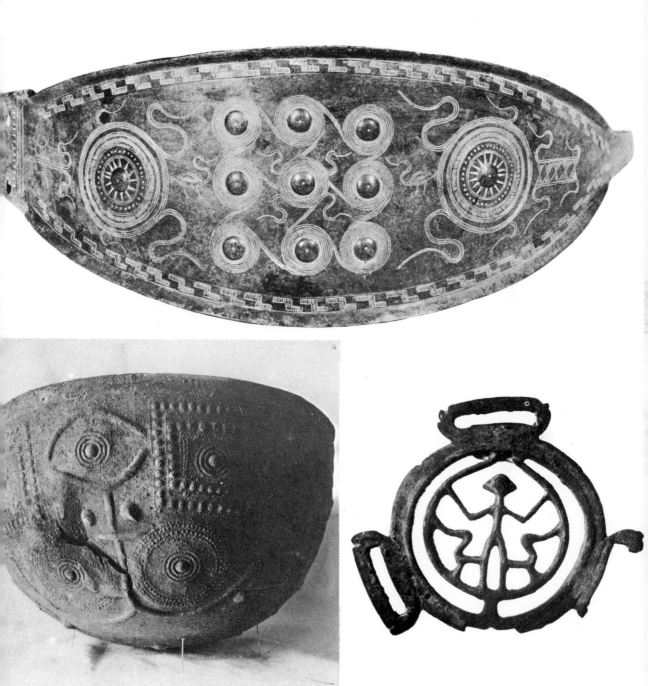

Top. Engraved bronze belt from Bologna. Eighth century B.C. *Left.* Bronze helmet decorated with a stylized face, from Tarquinia. Late eighth century B.C. *Right.* Bronze openwork disk with figures, from the handle of a vessel. Early seventh century B.C.

marked. An interesting tomb group from the Olmo Bello cemetery at Bisenzio, in Tarquinian country, includes a fine bronze vessel surmounted by groups of cast figures – a bear and a man dancing, a man leading a bullock – and a ladle with an upright handle has an openwork disc on top of it in the form of a human figure flanked by birds. The style is a less precise, half-understood, geometric Greek. At the same time, the importation of painted Greek geometric pottery inspires the beginnings of an art of painting in Etruria, especially in the southern area. The imitation of Greek geometric begins as early as 700 B.C.; it is competent but without much flair and the best work is probably done by immigrant craftsmen. Most of this early painted pottery comes from Tarquinia and its territory, Vulci, Veii and the Faliscan country.

In the seventh century, when the Etruscans were developing their characteristic city-civilization, and a wealthy aristocracy was established in most of the cities, the importation and manufacture of luxury *objets d'art* increased enormously. This is the age of the rich "orientalizing" tombs, of the Regolini-Galassi Tomb at Caere, of the Barberini Tomb at Palestrina, of the Vetulonia circle-tombs. Gold and silver, ivory, glass, fine bronze work are eagerly sought by the rich rulers of the cities. The Greeks, it seems, continued to be the chief carriers of foreign objects, but these included the products of many eastern countries – Anatolia, Syria, Phoenicia, Egypt and Cyprus. Local production of "orientalizing" objects quickly followed; a silver cup, it may be, of Corinthian shape decorated with friezes of strange animals, real and fantastic, from the oriental world; an ivory goblet with reliefs in similar style; an ostentatious and rather vulgar piece of gold jewellery of exquisite technique; a bronze cauldron with griffin heads or sirens attached to its rim. Much of this production is common to "orientalizing" art in Greece and Etruria, but the Etruscan work often has a genuinely independent character, especially the jewellery like the gold fibulae, sometimes of great size overloaded with ornament, engraved, stamped and moulded or decorated in the technique known as granulation in which patterns composed of minute granules of gold are applied to the surface.

It is important to assess the difference between this phase of artistic output in Etruria and the similar "orientalizing" phase in Greece. In Greece, oriental influence in the eighth and seventh centuries introduced a whole new repertory of formal and natural-istic patterns, but the reception of foreign ideas was accompanied by a flair, amounting to genius, for adapting them into an independent and disciplined artistic tradition. In Etruria the response is no less genuine, but its character is different, lacking the clear lines of independent development. We can assess it best, perhaps, on a humbler level, in the craft of pottery. The native pottery of the later seventh century is known as *bucchero* (plate 5), developed from the earlier "impasto" wares; it has a handsome black shiny surface produced by firing the clay in a closed kiln which turns the red ferric oxide of the clay into black ferrous oxide. *Bucchero* had some appeal even outside Etruria and was exported to several southern Greek colonies and to Carthage. It has turned up as far afield as Cyprus. The earliest *bucchero* shapes include graceful Corinthian cups, vessels of Rhodian shape initiated from metal versions, and Cypriot jugs also of metal origins; these are often decorated with engraved or low-relief ornament of oriental or Greek inspiration. At the same time, we find some remarkable *jeux d'esprit* inspired by a local taste for baroque ornamentation; outstanding are the group of vessels believed to come

Plate 13. Bronze vessel the Certosa (*situla*) with repoussé scenes showing a military parade, a funeral procession, and scenes of country life; found at Bologna. Early fifth century B.C. (Museo Civico, Bologna)

from the surrounding tombs of the Regolini-Galassi tumulus at Caere – a double vase in the form of two goat-birds, an extraordinary cup with a lid ornamented with bulls' heads and rams' heads, a vase with the foreparts of horses and the standing figure of a charioteer – which are products of an independent visual imagination.

It seems that the trade of Corinth dominated the Italian market from the second half of the seventh century. Typical Corinthian painted pottery was imported in enormous quantities, and locally imitated in the southern Etruscan cities. "Italo-Corinthian" has just one or two painters of individual character and just a few distinctive motifs, and even the best work stands far below the quality of its models. The tradition of Corinthian immigration into Etruria, represented by the person of Demaratus and his accompanying craftsmen, is well founded. The first "Italo-Corinthian" painters, may well have been immigrants. The Corinthian trade monopoly did not exclude the products, nor indeed the craftsmen, of other Greek places; some pottery from most Greek sources was coming in from the end of the seventh century, and in the last quarter of the seventh century there is evidence for craftsmen working locally in a style derived from the eastern Greek cities. Aristonothos, who painted the famous *krater* found at Caere, decorated with the Blinding of Polyphemus on one side and a sea-fight on the other, has been thought of as an artist from the Cyclades who had learnt his trade in Athens and had probably come to Etruria via the southern Greek colonies. An artist from the eastern Greek world working in Etruria around 630 B.C. made the cup illustrated on page 114. Certainly from the late seventh century there were very close and direct artistic contacts between Greece and Etruria which lasted until the early years of the fifth century and largely dictated the pattern of development of Etruscan art.

Around 600 B.C. we get the beginning of what may be called monumental art. The output of the seventh century had been confined to small-scale work, but Greece had been producing monumental religious sculpture since about 650 B.C. and some large-scale painting associated with the decoration of buildings. Stone sculpture in Etruria, like monumental architecture, has its origins in funerary practices. A series of male and female figures found in the Pietrera tumulus at Vetulonia, dating from around 600 B.C., apparently represent guardian deities protecting the tombs rather than humans; they are somewhat under life-sized and are carved in a Greco-Oriental style. Not long afterwards at Vulci there was a considerable output of funerary sculpture in the local stone: sphinxes (plate 6), centaurs, lions and other creatures made to protect and decorate the tombs; the style is Greek-inspired, some of the finer pieces being closely related to the so-called Dedalic style which prevailed in Greece in the later seventh century. At Clusium in the sixth century the ashes of the dead were often placed in a figure representing the dead person, life-size and sometimes over life-size. Clusium's output of ash urns, *cippi* and sarcophagi from about 540 B.C. onwards is famous; these objects, carved from local limestone in a delicate and precise "hellenizing" style, depict scenes of banquets, games, weddings and funerals which are important documents for the life and customs of the place. Stone sculpture in Etruria always remained predominantly funerary; there were plenty of good local stones but the marble of Carrara was not quarried, and stone was never used on a large scale for free-standing statuary nor in association with the architecture of buildings other than tombs. Temples continued to be built in wood and terracotta and cult-statues were of bronze or terracotta.

Plate 14. Bronze figure of the goddess Minerva. Early fifth century B.C.
(Galleria Nazionale Estense, Modena)

Above left. Painted vase with geometric decoration and figures, from Bisenzio. Early seventh century B.C.
Above right. Gold cup with figures of sphinxes on the handles, from the Bernardini Tomb, Praeneste. About 630 B.C. *Below.* Silver-gilt bowl from the Regolini-Galassi Tomb. Seventh century B.C.

Bronze griffin head with socketed end, once attached to a wooden pole. About 600 B.C.

Left. Stone torso of a woman, from the Pietrera Tomb, Vetulonia. Late seventh century B.C.
Right. Stone centaur from Vulci. Early sixth century B.C.

Terracotta sculpture has a unique place in the art of Etruria, and it was a branch of Etruscan art that was most genuinely admired in later times. Terracotta facings and free-standing sculpture played, as we have seen, a vital part in the structure and decoration of an Etruscan temple. There was, obviously, a great outburst of temple-building around the middle of the sixth century, especially in southern Etruria where Caere was one of the chief centres of fine terracotta work, and Veii had an important school which was to achieve fame in the person of Vulca of Veii, the only native Etruscan artist whose name has come down to us. He, we know, was commissioned to build the terracotta cult-statue for Rome's Temple of Jupiter. Although this branch of Etruscan art was heavily influenced from the beginning by Greek designs – the head-antefix, for example, was traditionally invented in Corinth, though it may have reached Etruria via southern Italy – Etruscan terracotta decoration is not without originality and is capable of outstanding achievements. The terracotta sculptors of the south produced

Above left. Bucchero vases from tombs in the Regolini-Galassi tumulus, Caere.
Left. Painted cup made by an East-Greek artist in Vulci. About 630 B.C.

some of their finest modelling in the last decades of the sixth century, when Etruscan art was strongly influenced by the art of the Ionian cities of Asia Minor. There are many fine figured friezes with a fairly wide range of subjects and some superb antefixes from Caere and Veii. Still outstanding among the south Etruscan terracottas are the figures which once decorated the Portonaccio temple at Veii, built about 500 B.C. The famous figure of Apollo from a group decorating the ridge of the roof, the theme of which was the struggle between Hercules and Apollo over the sacred hind, still typifies for many the independent achievement of the best Etruscan art, superficially Greek but fundamentally different in conception. The thrusting pose, the massive legs and thighs, the sharp intent profile of the face, the clinging drapery that adds strength to the massive

Terracotta antefix, from the Portonaccio temple at Veii. About 500 B.C.

The chimaera of Arezzo. About 350 B.C.

forms, express the creative experience of a truly Etruscan artist. It is not the Greek Apollo he has created but the Etruscan god of the same name.

The technique of hollow-casting large bronze figures became known in Greece in the sixth century and was probably introduced into Etruria not long afterwards. It was widely used for statues of gods and men. Very little Etruscan bronze work on a large scale has survived, and we are reminded of its fate, both in ancient and modern times, by the stories of how the Romans looted two thousand bronze statues from Volsinii in the third century B.C. and how Cardinal Farnese in 1546 contributed to the bronze decoration of the columns of S. Giovanni in Laterano a total of six thousand pounds of metal in complete and fragmentary ancient objects from the site of Tarquinia. The few survivors among big Etruscan bronze castings include two of the finest animal sculptures that have come down to us from ancient times, the well-known Capitoline wolf, made perhaps about 450 B.C., and the chimaera from Arezzo, perhaps a hundred years later.

For the rest, our knowledge of Etruscan bronze work down to 400 B.C. is mainly confined to small-scale votive bronzes and decorative craftsmanship from many cities. Tarquinia has yielded an interesting series of reliefs hammered from sheet bronze to decorate the walls of tombs; Caere, too, had a school of bronze workers to which a large group of hammered bronze reliefs found in the Perugia district has sometimes been attributed. It includes the famous tripods of S. Valentino di Marsciano and the reliefs from Castel S. Mariano which once decorated a splendid parade chariot. Around 540 Vulci came to be the centre of an industry producing fine votive bronzes and a wide range of domestic and religious objects with cast figures – tripods, censers, candelabra, vases and the like; Vulci's products were exported to most other Etruscan centres and outside Italy. Another important school grew up in Campania in the late sixth century, its centre apparently at Capua. Peculiar to Etruria is the series of bronze mirrors with engraved scenes, the drawing of which often rivals the best Greek drawing of the time. The mirrors are bronze discs with a projecting tang for insertion into a bone

Left. Bronze bowl and tripod stand decorated with repoussé figures, from Marsciano near Perugia. About 540 B.C. *Right*. Bronze stand with nude male figure as support. Made in Vulci. About 500 B.C.

Left. Bronze vessel with figures of mounted archers on the lid. Made in Campania. About 480 B.C.
Right. Detail of one of the archers

or wood handle; the reflecting surface is slightly convex and the drawing is on the concave back. The pictures are usually inspired by Greek legend, but there are some religious scenes and scenes of everyday life.

There are many fine Etruscan small bronze figures of the later sixth and early fifth centuries B.C. The differences between them and contemporary Greek work are easier to see than to describe, and few could be taken for anything other than Etruscan, whether they copy the guise of the Greek *kouroi* and *korai* or whether they are pure Etruscan types. Sometimes one sees a coarseness that marks provincial work wherever it may be, but, more often, it is something in the pose, some characteristically emphatic gesture of the hand, some expression of the face, some lack of balance or proportion. Typical of the best Etruscan work are the exquisitely finished figures of a male and female worshipper from Monteguragazza; the woman is closely modelled on a Greek *kore* but there is something typically Etruscan about her heavy-featured angular face. Another fine bronze figure of the early fifth century is the youth from Pizzirimonte in the British Museum (plate 15); his pose with feet together, left hand on hip and right extended forward, is purely Etruscan and he wears the typically Etruscan cloak, the *tebenna* which later developed into the Roman toga. Warriors, votaries, gods and goddesses are the chief subjects of these Etruscan small bronzes. There are some

Left. Bronze engraved mirror depicting a satyr and a maenad. About 470 B.C. *Right.* Bronze mirror with figures in low relief, showing Hercules carrying off Mlachuch. About 480 B.C.

superb little figures and groups associated with decorative bronze-work of the Vulcian school. A group (in the Metropolitan Museum of Art, New York) from the top of a candelabrum shows a warrior supporting a wounded comrade; the technique is exquisite, finely modelled and superbly finished, and the detailed genre scene is typically Etruscan.

The earliest examples of large-scale Etruscan painting belong to the years around 600 B.C. There are two early painted tombs at Caere, the *Circolo dei leoni dipinti* and the *Circolo degli animali dipinti*, and one of about the same time, the Campana Tomb, at Veii, and from this time onwards painting was widely practised in Etruria as a decorative art; we know it chiefly from painted tombs and temple decoration. Some fine painted terracotta plaques from the interior of a temple at Veii illustrate the high quality of painting associated with religious buildings, but such survivals are few. Our chief knowledge of Etruscan painting comes from the Tarquinian series of tombs, beginning about 550 B.C. (plates 7, 10, 11, 12). Tarquinian painted tombs have been known since the fifteenth century, but most of the famous ones were opened in the nineteenth century; recent discoveries, the result of electromagnetic soundings carried out by the

Lerici Foundation of Milan, have added some thirty-six new tombs, the majority of the archaic and classical periods. The paintings decorate the walls of rock-cut chamber-tombs, more modest than those of the "orientalizing" period, in the vast Monterozzi cemetery. Their purpose was, as we have seen, to recreate something of the atmosphere of domestic life, and the earliest tombs reproduce in some detail the interior forms of houses. Figure painting was, at first, confined to the triangular space created by the pitch of the ceiling and the horizontal crowning of the wall which was decorated with heraldic animals or small figure compositions. When decoration was extended to the walls of the chamber, there was usually a single figured frieze above an undecorated zone with the main part of the picture scheme on the end wall opposite the entrance.

In the earliest paintings, the paint was applied directly to the surface of the rock, later to a layer of plaster; the technique is sometimes true fresco with the paint applied to wet plaster, while sometimes the painting was not done until the plaster had dried. The artist prepared his design by drawing or incising its outlines, and had at his disposal a fair range of colours – red, white, black, yellow, green and blue – derived from earths and organic substances. The colours were applied, as in early Greek paintings, as flat washes filling the outlines of the drawing; the colour-schemes are largely conventional and frankly decorative. Mixed colours and gradations of tone are introduced in some of the late archaic pictures. One of the earliest Tarquinian tombs, the recently discovered Capanna tomb, is without figured decoration, but soon figures appear in the triangular space and, in the decade 540–530, on the main walls. From the first the paintings are strikingly decorative; Tomb 3698 has a splendid pair of tomb-guardians flanking the consoles that support the ridge-beam; on the right is a lion, his background legs half red, half green, and his mane and underside blue; on the left is a panther in a similar colour-scheme. All the best figure scenes are lively and colourful, extremely convincing in their rendering of the movement and gesture of the dance and often highly dramatic in the handling of scenes of violent action. Exceptional is the series of pictures in the Tomb of Hunting and Fishing where nature, keenly observed, has inspired an excitingly colourful interpretation.

It is worth stressing again that in the late sixth and early fifth centuries, the contacts between Greek and Etruscan artists were close and direct, both in the southern colonies and in Etruria proper. We have already seen that the first painters in the Italo-Corinthian style were probably Greek, and there can hardly be any doubt that Athenians were responsible for the first creditable black-figure pottery, the so-called Pontic vases, based on Athenian models and showing, at first, a fine technique and an assured handling of mythological scenes but declining later into indifferent craftsmanship and confused subject-matter. It was quite certainly an Ionian Greek who set up shop in Caere around 540 B.C. to make a special kind of vessel for carrying liquids and produced a series of handsome, richly polychrome vases with racy versions of Greek mythology, especially stories about Hercules, an Etruscan favourite. One likes to think of this artist, some forty or more of whose works are known, as completely at home in the Etruscan milieu and deriving genuine inspiration from it. Striking similarities between Caeretan *hydriae*, as they are called (plate 8), and tomb-paintings from Tarquinia, for example those of the Tomb of the Augurs, have often been noticed, and although one would hesitate to attribute the tomb paintings, which are so deeply

Left. Bronze figure of a woman, from Monteguragazza. Early fifth century B.C. *Right.* Painted clay vessel of so-called Pontic type, made in Etruria; the lower frieze shows a banquet scene. About 540 B.C.

Left. Terracotta head of a youth, from Veii. About 460 B.C. *Right.* Bronze statuette of a javelin-thrower. About 490 B.C.

concerned with Etruscan ideology, to a Greek artist, there is no doubt that the presence of Greek artists was a dominating influence on their style. Opinion, indeed, is seriously divided about the nationality of the artists who made many of the outstanding works of Etruscan art, but in all branches of that art we find examples which we could readily attribute to Greek craftsmanship. It is hard to believe that some of the finest engraved mirrors, the best intaglios and many other things were not made for Etruscan patrons by resident Greek craftsmen.

The decades after 500 B.C. were, as we have seen, the turning-point in the fortunes of the Etruscan states, marked by the breakdown of some of their most direct Greek contacts. Among Tarquinian paintings, the Tomb of the Chariots brings us to the high point of Greek influence; we seem to see there a genuine sympathy and understanding of Greek ideals in the fine pictures from the tomb, strongly disciplined by the Greek sense of form. How close and direct Greek contacts were in this period may also be seen in many terracotta sculptures from the southern cities which show the influence of the style that inaugurated the classical revolution in Greece in the years after 480 B.C. Superb terracottas in this style have been found in southern Etruria and Latium, most recently the magnificent figure-groups from a temple at Pyrgi which owe much to the

Left. Terracotta group of Athena and Zeus fighting with giants. From Temple B at Pyrgi. About 480 B.C. *Right.* Fragment of a terracotta group of a maenad and a satyr. 470–460 B.C.

style of the Olympian sculptures. A bronze statuette of a nude athlete in Paris reveals the same intense interest in human anatomy as a Greek work of the time, and something of the same nobility of form and strongly-knit athletic ideal

But after, say, 460 B.C. the picture changes, chiefly because there was no longer a large-scale immigration of craftsmen from the city-states of Greece. The traditional techniques of painting, bronze-casting and terracotta modelling maintain high standards of craftsmanship but without the direct influence of artists from Greece, so that even the best work maintains an archaic appearance long after the archaic style had disappeared in Greece itself. The vase illustrated on page 125 was made in imitation of Athenian red-figure pottery by applying red paint to the surface and engraving the internal details. The date is around 460 B.C., but there are many details in the figures that recall the style of Athenian vase-painters active thirty years earlier. A work like the bronze figure of a warrior in Florence, dating from the mid-fifth century (plate 16), still has the arrogant archaic pose, and many of the conventions of archaic dress are combined with something like a classical profile, but there is no hint of the relaxed

Left. Clay vase with figures applied in red paint, to imitate the Athenian red-figure technique. About 460 B.C. *Right*. Bronze figure of a horseman. About 440 B.C.

balance and studied symmetry of a contemporary Greek work. In the second half of the fifth century some influence of the developed classical style can be seen in many local works, but there is always something characteristically Etruscan. The bronze rider in Detroit, a work of about 440–430 B.C., combines the relaxation and powerful modelling of a classical Greek bronze with clear-cut archaic features in the face and drapery. It is typical of the period.

It is arguable that the Etruscan artistic vision which could make a genuine response to the schematic forms of archaic Greek art could never have come to terms completely with the harmony and discipline of the Greek fifth-century ideal. There is a strong element of truth in this view, but it must be remembered that there were also historical reasons for the failure of Greek classicism to make the same creative impact in Etruria, apart from innate differences of artistic expression. All we can say with certainty is that the full influence of classical art is not seen in Etruria until long after the classical style had been developed in Greece. There are some fragments of terracotta sculpture from a temple at Orvieto which recall the art of Pheidias, and others from Falerii in the

Ager Faliscus; both groups date from around 400 B.C. Orvieto was a cosmopolitan city and the Faliscan territory had close ties with Rome which by now was beginning to usurp the power of the south Etruscan cities. Greek influence may have reached here through Rome which, according to the literary tradition, had a number of direct contacts with Greek cities in the fifth century; but it was not until the later fourth century that the art of the Greeks again produced a widespread creative response in central Italy.

Plate 15. Bronze figure of a young man wearing a cloak. From Pizzirimonte. Early fifth century B.C. (British Museum, London)

Chapter Nine

LANGUAGE

The study of the Etruscan language has been long and not unprofitable, but it remains the most difficult aspect of Etruscan studies and the main stumbling-block to a real, deep understanding of this ancient people. We now have an enormous, and ever increasing, number of documents in Etruscan, well over ten thousand inscriptions on stone, pottery, bronze and other materials ranging in date from the middle of the seventh century to the first century B.C., not only from the homeland of Etruria but also from other parts of Italy which were colonized or influenced by the Etruscans. In 1893 it was decided to prepare a systematic edition of the known texts and the *Corpus Inscriptionum Etruscarum* was begun; after an initial burst, it has progressed rather slowly and a very high proportion of Etruscan texts remain unedited, though the most important new discoveries are carefully recorded and often analysed in detail in the Italian *Studi Etruschi* and other periodicals. We still lack a thorough lexical index of the language, though one is in preparation; recently an attempt was made to produce an index of words and frequencies with the aid of a computer in Wisconsin. Although progress in the understanding of the language has been made, it must be admitted that some of the most recently discovered texts have often presented insoluble difficulties of interpretation.

We do not know when the people of Etruria began to speak Etruscan but we do know approximately when they began to write it down. The earliest inscriptions in the language belong to about the middle of the seventh century and they were written in an alphabet which, like all ancient alphabets, derives from the north Semitic; it is generally believed that this alphabet was adopted not much earlier. The most important document for the origins of writing in Etruria is the alphabet engraved on the edge of an ivory writing tablet found at Marsiliana d'Albegna in a context which would date it to about 650 B.C.; it is usually taken as the prototype Etruscan alphabet. The Etruscan alphabet of Marsiliana contains twenty-two north Semitic letters and four additions made by the Greeks: $\Phi X \Psi \Omega$. From this it is deduced that the Etruscans got it from a Greek source. It is possible to argue further. About a hundred years before, the Greeks themselves had adopted the north Semitic alphabet and adapted it to the sounds of their own language; shortly, two main types were evolved distinguished by the values which they gave to X and Ψ and the order in which the letters $X \Phi \Psi$ appeared in the alphabet. Etruscan is related to the group of western, or red, alphabets in which $X = ks$ (or ξ) and $\Psi = kh$ (or X) and the order of letters is $X \Phi \Psi$. This is basically the type of alphabet used by the Cumaeans who were the nearest Greek neighbours of the Etruscans, so it is tempting to think that Cumae was the source from which the Etruscans of the seventh century learnt to write. This is the view, a most plausible one,

Plate 16. Bronze figure of the god Mars, or of a warrior. About 440 B.C. (Museo Archeologico, Florence)

129

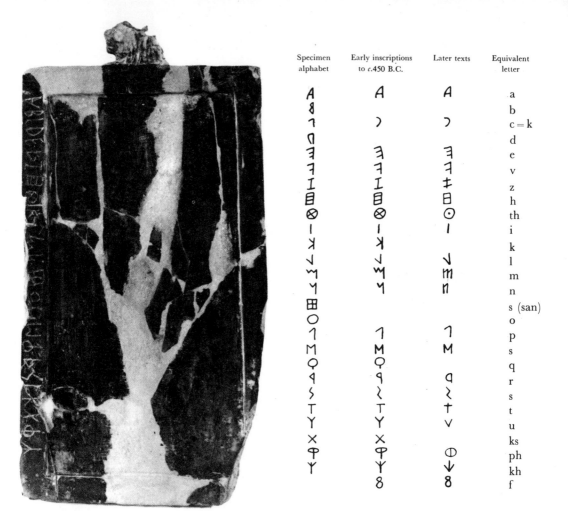

Specimen alphabet	Early inscriptions to c.450 B.C.	Later texts	Equivalent letter
			a
			b
			c = k
			d
			e
			v
			z
			h
			th
			i
			k
			l
			m
			n
			s (san)
			o
			p
			s
			q
			r
			s
			t
			u
			ks
			ph
			kh
			f

Left. Ivory writing tablet from the Circolo degli Avori, Marsiliana d'Albegna. Seventh century B.C. *Right.* The Etruscan alphabet and its development

which is generally held today. The only difficulty is that one Etruscan letter of north Syrian origin, *san*, is not found in any Cumaean inscription, the earliest of which date from before 700 B.C., and this has led some scholars to argue a mixed origin for the Etruscan alphabet. Support for this view comes from the fact that seventh-century Etruscan culture seems to have been open to influences from a wide variety of sources. But it is perhaps more likely that this Phoenician letter survived in the specimen alphabet of the Cumaeans, from which the Etruscans would have learnt, though it did not, in fact, appear in their inscriptions. Obviously the alphabet, as it was first acquired, attained a sort of magical significance, and indeed the Etruscans themselves continued for some time to write their *abecedaria* with letters which did not correspond with sounds in their own language and were not used in their own texts.

The prototype alphabet was maintained, in fact, down to the fifth century though the Etruscans by then had no use for *san*, nor for *beta*, *delta*, *kappa* and *quoppa*. Because their speech knew no distinction between the sounds of b and p, d and t, k and g, the

Early *bucchero* cup with inscription round the base, from the Tomba del Duce, Vetulonia

letters b, d, and k disappeared altogether from use and c was used for the sounds of g and k. The Etruscans did, however, add one letter to the alphabet they received; this is the letter 8=f which appears already in some of the earliest inscriptions such as that on the tombstone of Avele Feluske at Vetulonia. Its origin remains quite uncertain. In the fifth century the alphabet still had three signs for s, and a total of twenty-three letters, but later on one of the s-signs, together with k and g, went out, so that by about 400 B.C. there were twenty letters with four vowels and sixteen consonants. The main changes in the alphabet during this period from 650 to 400 are shown on page 130. After 650 B.C. the spread of writing was fairly rapid in Etruria; it was not for long confined to a small class nor was it a restricted craft. The use of an alphabet, much simpler than a cumbersome syllabary with ideograms like the Mycenaean Linear B, facilitates the rapid spread of literacy and there are plenty of inscriptions on quite humble objects, often creditably calligraphic, in the seventh and sixth centuries from many parts of Etruria. Elegant inscriptions, sometimes in ornamental frames or written in patterns, are often the chief decorative motif on early vases and suggest a prominence given to the written word and probably a magical significance. From Etruria knowledge of alphabetic writing spread to most parts of Italy and all the alphabets of ancient Italy as far as the south Alpine regions are essentially derived from the Etruscan.

We may suppose that by 600 B.C. writing was widely known in Etruria and employed for many uses in administration, commerce, education, and religion. The texts on perishable materials, including linen-paged books and scrolls, have disappeared; what survive are inscriptions on stone and pottery and other permanent media. They were not generally of great length and are predominantly funerary in character, but there are a few longer ones, including one or two important religious texts, of the period with which we are concerned. Since the seventeenth century these texts have been the object of study by scholars and amateurs; many of them, especially the shorter funerary inscriptions, can be read with fair ease, but we are still a long way from a complete understanding of the language as a whole; it is still a fruitful ground for fantasy and wild conjecture. Here we can do no more than indicate the basis of our knowledge and try to give some account of what has been achieved.

Throughout classical antiquity some knowledge of the Etruscan language survived; it was still spoken in parts of Etruria and known to contemporary Roman scholars. A number of ancient authors give us the Etruscan equivalents for Latin and Greek words; some sixty such equivalents are known and constitute an important element in our knowledge of Etruscan vocabulary. They include the names of the months from March to October, the word for a gladiator-trainer (*lanista*), for a king (*lucumo*), for a flute-player (*subulo*). From our knowledge of the Latin language we can add a little that the ancients left unsaid, since several words look like having an Etruscan origin, such as *caerimonia* and even, perhaps, *miles*, a soldier. Latin words of ultimately Greek derivation, by the changes in the vowels and consonants, often betray an Etruscan mediation: θρίαμβος – *triumpus* – triumph; γνῶμα – *gruma* – a surveying instrument; κίστη– *cisterna* – a box; and the like. Perhaps even the cognomen of the great Horatius who held the bridge against Porsenna of Clusium is Etruscan, for *Cocles*, the one-eyed, looks suspiciously like an Etruscan version of the Greek Cyclops. These Etruscan origins for many Latin words reflect the great contribution of Etruria to early Rome which was evident in every sphere of Roman life.

But our main knowledge of the language has been gained from the Etruscan texts themselves. The most immediately informative class of documents are the bilingual Etruscan-Latin texts, all of which are comparatively late, from the third century B.C. onwards, and mostly short funerary inscriptions. They have established, or at least, confirmed, the meanings of several words which commonly appear in funerary formulae. Another class of inscriptions which are in effect bilinguals are those engraved on bronze mirrors and other objects accompanying Greek mythological scenes whose subject is obvious; the word *hinthial*, meaning shade, accompanies the shade of Teiresias in an underworld scene. Etruscan versions of Greek names, though they do not add to the vocabulary, are important for what they tell us of Etruscan phonetics, for they show considerable variation in the rendering of Greek vowels and consonants, and a strong tendency to what is known as vowel harmony, or the tendency to repeat the same vowel in adjacent syllables, so that the Greek Κλυταιμνγ̇στρα, for example, becomes

Cluthumnustha, an equivalence which also shows the well-known Etruscan tendency to aspirate certain of the consonants. A long bilingual, if one such were found, would inevitably constitute a great advance in Etruscan studies. The three sheets of gold leaf found recently at Pyrgi, the port of Caere, hold new hope for the future. Two of the inscriptions are in Etruscan and one in Punic, but neither of the Etruscan texts appears to be the exact counterpart of the Punic and there are, unfortunately, some difficulties about the text of the Punic. So far the chief value of this find has been as a historical document, but its possibilities for the translation of the language are by no means exhausted.

Without the aid of bilinguals the problems of translating the lengthier Etruscan texts seem almost insuperable. The present position is that the phonetic values of the words in any inscription are certain, but that the known vocabulary is still small and much of the syntax of the language quite uncertain. The language is written generally from right to left, occasionally boustrophedon (i.e. back and forth, as the ox ploughs) and sometimes from left to right. A fundamental problem is that of punctuation. The early inscriptions show no breaks between words and the punctuation system which was adopted in the seventh century is still not fully understood; it is not a word punctuation but serves to separate syllables or groups of letters. In some inscriptions dots, either single or a number arranged vertically, appear to be purely decorative. Dividing the early inscriptions into their component words is often difficult, involving several possibilities; this is one main reason why a number of inscriptions of the archaic period have proved particularly difficult to interpret.

The general approach to the problem of interpreting documents has changed over the years, but two fundamentally different methods may be distinguished. The first attempts to find grammatical and other parallels with known languages, originally Indo-European tongues and, when these prove unfruitful, with a wider range of linguistic groups. The second method, which has provided steady but unspectacular results, concerns itself with the comparison of the various texts, examining the words and combinations of words in different contexts, and so building up both the vocabulary and the morphology of the language. There is nothing wrong intrinsically with the first method; the trouble has been its uncritical application without a clear under-standing of the phonetic system and structure of the Etruscan language. We have been shown a wide variety of comparisons between Etruscan words and many European languages, most recently and notoriously Albanian, but none of these comparative etymologies convince reputable scholars. Even the more restrained and well-founded comparisons hardly stand a searching test. A Russian scholar has recently tried to demonstrate that Etruscan is an Indo-European language, and that many of its words are closely related to Greek. We know, indeed, that many loan words were adopted from Greek and from other neighbouring languages, but very few of the less obvious comparisons are acceptable; and it is impossible to find any convincing morphological connections between Greek and Etruscan. The result of such attempts has been that most scholars have now fallen back on the position held by Dionysius of Halicarnassus who said that Etruscan was like no other known language. They would not deny that it has elements derived from a number of Indo-European dialects and many loan words from Greek and Latin but they would claim that it is a fundamentally different tongue.

Their conclusion would be that internal comparison of the various texts is, at present, the only one likely to produce valid results.

This is, in fact, the method which since the eighteenth century has been chiefly responsible for the advance made in our knowledge of Etruscan. The bulk of the known vocabulary has come from the frequent occurrence of certain words in certain types of contexts. *Ril* meaning age, *clan* meaning son, *puia* meaning daughter, often occur in funerary inscriptions, though mostly of a later date than the period dealt with here. From dedicatory inscriptions on a wide variety of objects we get a large number of roots such as *tur-*, *mul-*, *scu-*, which have different shades of meaning associated with the making of offerings, though the shades of meaning are not always understood. From the same source we learn something of the different tenses of the verb and of case endings of the noun – the genitives in *-al* and *-si*, the locative in *-thi*. Sometimes two or three syllables are added to the root: *uni-al* means "of Uni" (the goddess Juno), *uni-al-thi* means "in Juno's temple or sanctuary". The precise meaning of many of the suffixes and their combination is still not established. There is a good deal of evidence for the numerals in Etruscan; the numbers 1–6 are written on the faces of a pair of dice from Tuscania, now in the Bibliothèque Nationale, Paris, but there is some doubt as to their exact order. The most widely accepted equivalence is: *thu* = 1, *zal* = 2, *ci* = 3, *sa* = 4, *mach* = 5, *huth* = 6; multiples of 10 are formed by the addition of the suffix *-alch*, 30 being *cialch* and 40 *sealch*.

An examination of some texts will give a general idea of the state of knowledge of the language. A simple dedicatory inscription such as that engraved on a *bucchero* vase from Caere presents no difficulty. It reads *mini mulvanice Mamarce Velchanas. Mini* is the

Pair of numbered dice, from Tuscania

oblique or accusative case of the first person pronoun *mi* meaning "I", *mulvanice* is the past tense, the aorist, from the root *mul* which means "dedicate" or the like; Mamarce is the Christian name of the man, his *praenomen*, Italic rather than Etruscan, Velchanas is his family name, his *nomen*. So the inscription is translated "Mamarce Velchanas dedicated me". A variant occurs on a sixth-century *bucchero* vase from Ischia di Castro: *mine muluvene avile acvilnas*, suggesting dialectal variations in the form of the verb and the pronoun, though there is generally much uncertainty in the rendering of Etruscan vowels. Slightly more complicated and difficult is the inscription on a *bucchero* amphora of Nikosthenic shape from the Monte Abatone cemetery at Caere: *mi aranth ramuthasi vestiricinala muluvanice*. The morphology of two words here is uncertain; *ramuthasi* is probably a genitive meaning "(son) of Ramutha", and *vestiricinala* a woman's name in the dative, indicating the person to whom the object was offered. But alternatives are possible.

The shorter, or B, text from the sanctuary at Pyrgi, illustrates well the limits of achievement in the translation of the language. It commemorates a ritual act and is comparatively simple in its forms, but a large number of doubtful elements remain in the interpretation so far achieved. It reads: *nac . thefarie . veliiunas . thamuce . cleva . etanal . masan . tiurunias . selace . vacal . tmial . avilchval . amuce . pulumchva . snuiaph*. The name of Thefarie Velianas, which occurs on the A inscription as well, is that of the chief magistrate, perhaps the tyrant of Caere around 450 B.C., the date to which the inscription belongs; and we know that the text deals with his dedications which were commemorated in the three gold plaques. Of the words in the inscription, *nac* appears to mean "thus"; *thamuce*, *selace* and *amuce* are three of the well-known dedicatory words

Three inscribed gold plaques found at Pyrgi. Fifth century B.C.

not precisely defined, all in the past tense; *cleva* which also occurs on the Capua tile is apparently a kind of offering; *masan tiurunias* almost certainly means "in the month of Masan", *tiurs* being understood to mean "moon" from other inscriptions; *vacal tmial avilchval amuce* is a combination of words, all more or less known but not in their exact significance; *vacal* is common in other texts and means an offering or sacrifice; and *avil* is known from many funerary texts to mean "year". The last two words are quite uncertain. The result is that all we can do with this inscription is to establish the general gist which seems to be that Thefarie Velianas has made offerings in the month of Masan, and perhaps established an annual religious ceremony of some kind.

One of the most important of early inscriptions is the sixth-century *cippus* now in Perugia which appears to be the text of an agreement between two local families over the boundaries of land. It comes from Monte Gualandro to the north of Lake Trasimene, probably in Cortona's territory. In a case like this when the words and the subject-matter are both unfamiliar, the translation of the text is immensely difficult. The preamble of the *cippus* reads:

> *(t)eurat . tanna . la . rezus*
> *ame vachr lautn . velthinas . e*
> *stla . afunas sleleth caru*
> *tezan . fusleri . lesns teis*
> *rasnes . ipa ama hen naper*
> *XII . velthinathuras . cras . pe*
> *ras cemulm lescul zuci . en*
> *esci . epl tularu*

The interpretation is largely conjectural, all that can be said with certainty being that the families involved are the *Velthina* and the *Afuna*. *Lautn* is the root for family, and a few other words can be given approximate meanings; the relative pronoun *ipa*, *caru* "to make", and so on. It is tempting to consider the words *fusleri lesns teis rasnes* as a formula meaning "in accordance with Etruscan law" or something similar, since *rasn-* is certainly the root meaning the people of Etruria; it occurs in several other inscriptions, and ancient authors record that the Etruscans called themselves *Rasenna*.

The longest inscription so far found on a pottery vessel occurs on a little *bucchero* aryballos of Corinthian shape, probably found at Caere; it is called the Poupé aryballos and dates from the late seventh century. The inscription is engraved on the body of the vase, going round it from left to right and from top to bottom in $4\frac{1}{2}$ turns. It illustrates the complexities of the early system of punctuation and the enormity of the problem of interpretation of the lengthier texts. Its 181 letters are written as follows: *zusatunin . aatiuth: arvasaapha . nuvathima . suvemmanichiur: al . aalchuvaiseraturannuvei . nelusisnialthuiu . ri . athi . litiltalipilekatur . anuvecemima – – – matesi . araturanuve . velusi . na echethaiarai . naa . siikanzich: akarai.* It will be noticed that there are several single stops in the punctuation and three double stops; they do not necessarily mean breaks between words and clearly the groups of letters between stops often consist of several words. The double stops must surely be definitive breaks in the text. Very few of the words in this important inscription are in fact understood; *aisera* is from the root *ais-* meaning "god" as an ancient gloss informs us; *turannuve* ought to be connected with the goddess *turan* who was identified with the Greek Aphrodite but *nuve* may be a separate

Inscribed *cippus* from Perugia

word or the ending of a compound form; *zich* is certainly the root meaning to write and is fairly common.

The results so far achieved in the interpretation of longer Etruscan texts mean that the general purport of some of them can be made out but that great uncertainties remain in the vocabulary and syntax. The Capua tile with its 60 lines of which some 30 are legible appears to preserve a funerary ritual with prescriptions for sacrifice to the gods of the underworld, extracted, it may be, from the *Libri Acheruntici*. The Perugia *cippus*, whether funerary or not, contains details of a division of land between two families. The curious Magliano lead inscription with its spiral text is a ritual document giving the names of several gods among whom the chief god *Tins* or *Tinia* is clearly recognizable. The essential content of the Pyrgi inscriptions is known. We have some knowledge of the grammar of the language, a limited vocabulary, a good understanding of its phonetics and phonetic development from early to later times. We still do not understand its relation to other Mediterranean languages, though it is obvious that it shares a number of terminations and roots with the sixth-century language of Lemnos and some with Lycian and Lydian. The similarities with Lemnian are sometimes very striking: the Lemnian *zivai aviz sialchviz marazm* may be compared with the *zivas avils xxvi* of a late Etruscan funerary text, and *-alch* is the suffix used in Etruscan to denote multiples of ten. The general view is still that Etruscan belongs in some way to a Mediterranean substratum of languages of pre-Indo-European formation, though, obviously, some elements show the influence of Indo-European forms.

It is clear that with the publication of more texts through the *Corpus Inscriptionum Etruscarum* and by other means, and with the application of modern methods of linguistic study, knowledge of the language will rapidly improve. In the meantime the interest and variety of the theme is stressed by what has already been learnt of dialectal variations in the inscriptions from different parts of Italy – from Campania, coastal Etruria, and the interior. Pallottino's analysis of the sixth-century inscriptions from Orvieto shows a distinct dialectal character linking them with the forms of later Etruscan elsewhere, for example the genitive form in *-al* instead of *-a*. It is suspected that a common literary language was developed quite early, as the result of the systematization of religious texts at religious meetings of the Etruscan states. There is some suggestion of a literary language in the Capua tile, and of metrical forms in the early dedicatory inscriptions. These intriguing features are only hinted at in our present knowledge of the texts.

Donald Strong is Assistant Keeper of Greek and Roman Antiquities at the British Museum. He is the author of a number of books on Greek and Roman art and archaeology, and wrote the section on the Etruscans in *Vanished Civilizations*, edited by Edward Bacon.

CONCLUSION

"If you try to make a grand amalgam of Cerveteri and Tarquinia, Vulci, Vetulonia, Volterra, Clusium, Veii, then you won't get the essential Etruscan as a result, but a cooked up mess which has no life-meaning at all." So D. H. Lawrence at his most persuasive towards the end of his book *Etruscan Places*. The Etruscans, he claimed, are an experience and he did not want to be instructed in them. The confident enjoyment of life on earth and the sure hope of a life after death which the aristocracy of Etruria so strikingly revealed in the paintings of their tombs, became for Lawrence an unambitious and uninhibited devotion to enjoyment. It became so because Lawrence felt obliged to explain what others might call the "failure" of the Etruscans.

At the end of the period dealt with in this book, the Etruscans were beginning to succumb to "outlandish warriors armed with strange weapons" who came upon them from the north and to the military efficiency of the Romans. There was treachery at Clusium, political dissension and tyranny at Veii, incompetence at Volsinii, disunity in Etruria as a whole. It is easy to find reasons for this apparent failure – luxury and effeminacy, a morbidly superstitious religion, an unhealthy social and political organization or, simply, as Lawrence preferred, the lack of a will to succeed in the sense that history measures success. But, in truth, there was no failure. The Etruscans, if they remained barbarians in the eyes of the Greeks, did more than any other Mediterranean people to transmit Greek thought and culture. If there were elements of cruelty, sensuality, magic and blind superstition, these were elements common to primitive humanity and perhaps to humanity for ever. The Romans who overwhelmed the Etruscans did not make the mistake of underestimating them. Their greatest historian, Livy, observed how the kings of Rome, among whom were a number of Etruscans, "nursed our strength and enabled us ultimately to produce sound fruit from liberty, ensuring a politically adult nation".

The Etruscans did not fail; on the contrary, they achieved considerable success in the art of living. Their reputation has suffered most from their decline. No glorious moment ended the rule of the Etruscans in Italy. One by one their cities fell to Rome and soon their peasantry began to leave a once fertile countryside. And then the cities and towns became deserted as the patterns of settlement changed under Roman rule. The Etruscan soothsayer became a figure of fun; impoverished Etruscan town-dwellers got a reputation for squalor and immorality. The vision of a glorious past faded. That past has never been so dramatically re-created as it was for the Minoans, with whom the Etruscans often seem to have much in common. They have no Evans and, as yet, no Ventris. But if many aspects of their life and thought remain mysterious, we now have a much clearer picture of their role in history and of the elements of greatness in these forerunners of the Romans.

BIBLIOGRAPHY

Readers of English will find it difficult to pursue Etruscan studies far in their own language. They have, it is true, the greatest book written about the Etruscans in George Dennis's *Cities and Cemeteries of Etruria*, the third edition of which appeared in 1883; of all books it is still the best to choose as a companion when touring Etruria. They also have a great writer's personal confession of faith in the Etruscan people in D. H. Lawrence's *Etruscan Places* (London, 1932). But the English-speaking countries have produced few Etruscologists in recent times and the bulk of English reading on the subject is made up of translations of important works by foreign scholars. M. Pallottino's *The Etruscans* (Pelican, 1955) is a translation of his *Etruscologia* first published in 1942 and, although still valuable, has been superseded by later Italian editions, the most recent of which appeared in 1963. This last contains very full bibliographical references. J. Heurgon's *La Vie Quotidienne chez les Etrusques* (Paris, 1961), has recently been translated into English. E. H. Richardson's *The Etruscans* (Chicago, 1964) is another general account of the subject which also has a fairly comprehensive bibliography. L. Banti's *Il Mondo degli Etruschi* (Rome, 1960), is an important recent book which has not yet appeared in English.

A number of books on Etruscan art have been published in English, including P. J. Riis, *An Introduction to Etruscan Art* (1953); M. Pallottino, *Art of the Etruscans* (1958); and G. A. Mansuelli, *Etruria and Early Rome* (1966). M. Pallottino's *Etruscan Painting* (1952) is the most up-to-date general work on the subject, but appeared before the most recent Tarquinian discoveries which are described in M. Moretti's *Nuovi monumenti della pittura Etrusca* (1966). The most valuable general studies of Etruscan art are still P. Ducati's *Storia dell' Arte Etrusca* (1927) and G. Giglioli's *L'Arte Etrusca* (1935), both of which have a large number of black-and-white illustrations of the most important Etruscan works. J. D. Beazley's *Etruscan Vase-Painting* (1947) discusses various aspects of Etruscan painted pottery.

There is no book in English on the Etruscan language. References to foreign publications will be found in the general works cited above. Pallottino's *Elementi di lingua Etrusca* (1936), though somewhat outdated, is still valuable and his *Testimonia Linguae Etruscae* is the most accessible collection of important Etruscan texts. The *Corpus Inscriptionum Etruscarum* which was begun in 1898 is still being actively compiled.

Recent Etruscan discoveries are chronicled chiefly in the annual publication *Studi Etruschi* which first appeared in 1927 on the founding of the Institute of Etruscan and Italian Studies in Florence. Important excavation and field-work is also reported in *Notizie degli Scavi* and in the journals of various foreign academies in Italy.

ACKNOWLEDGEMENTS

Plates 2, 5, 8 and 15 and the illustrations on pages 57, 88 and 93 are from photographs (© George Rainbird Ltd 1968) taken for this book by Derrick Witty in the Department of Greek and Roman Antiquities at the British Museum by kind permission of the Keeper.

For permission to reproduce copyright illustrations, grateful acknowledgements are made to:
Alinari: pages 22, 85, 90 *bottom*, 114 *top*, 115 *right*, 116
Antikensammlungen, Munich: page 118 *left* and *right*
Archives Photographiques, Caisse Nationale des Monuments Historiques, Paris: page 106
Bibliothèque Nationale, Paris: page 134
British Museum: pages 20 *right*, 49 *right*, 83 *right*, 107 *bottom right*, 113, 120 *right*, 125 *left*
British School at Rome: page 31
F. Bruckmann: page 86
J. Allan Cash: page 48
Detroit Institute of Arts: page 125 *right*
J. Felbermeyer: page 124
Fototeca Unione, Rome: pages 37, 75, 135
Galleria Nationale Estense, Modena: plate 14
Professor A. Giuliano: page 114 *bottom*
Italian State Tourist Office: page 36
C. Lerici: page 91
City of Liverpool Museums: page 103
Mansell Collection: pages 43 *left*, 59, 78, 105 *left*, 119 *left* and *right*, endpapers
Metropolitan Museum of Art, New York: pages 43 *right*, 122 *right*
Musée du Louvre: page 123 *right*
Museo Archeologico Nazionale dell'Umbria, Perugia: page 137
Museo Civico, Piacenza: page 94
Museo Civico Archeologico, Bologna: plate 13; pages 107 *top*, 122 *left*
Museum für Kunst und Gewerbe, Hamburg: page 54 *left*
National Museum, Copenhagen: page 69
Ny Carlsberg Glyptotek, Copenhagen: plate 4; pages 123 *left*, 124 *right*
Sacco: page 84 *left* and *right*
Soprintendenza alle Antichità dell'Etruria, Florence: pages 15, 20 *left*, 25 *bottom*, 54 *right*, 83 *left*, 102 *top*, 107 *bottom left*, 112 *top left*, 115 *left*, 117, 130 *left*, 131
Scala: plates 1, 3, 6, 7, 9, 10, 11, 12, 14, 16
Staatliche Museen, Berlin: page 102 *bottom*
Staatliche Museen der Stiftung Preussischer Kulturbesitz, Berlin: page 105 *right*
Vatican Museum: pages 24, 25 *top*, 112 *bottom*
Victoria & Albert Museum, London: page 120 *left*
Villa Giulia Museum, Rome: page 112 *top right*

INDEX

The page numbers in *italic type* indicate illustrations